how to
Write
your own
Living
Will

HOW TO WRITE YOUR OWN LIVING WILL

Fourth Edition

———

Edward A. Haman
Attorney at Law

SPHINX® PUBLISHING
AN IMPRINT OF SOURCEBOOKS, INC.®
NAPERVILLE, ILLINOIS
www.SphinxLegal.com

Fourth Edition: 2004
Second Printing: June, 2004

Published by: **Sphinx® Publishing, An Imprint of Sourcebooks, Inc.®**

Naperville Office
P.O. Box 4410
Naperville, Illinois 60567-4410
630-961-3900
Fax: 630-961-2168
www.sourcebooks.com
www.SphinxLegal.com

This publication is designed to provide accurate and authoritative information in regard to the subject matter covered. It is sold with the understanding that the publisher is not engaged in rendering legal, accounting, or other professional service. If legal advice or other expert assistance is required, the services of a competent professional person should be sought.

From a Declaration of Principles Jointly Adopted by a Committee of the
American Bar Association and a Committee of Publishers and Associations

This product is not a substitute for legal advice.

Disclaimer required by Texas statutes.

Library of Congress Cataloging-in-Publication Data
Haman, Edward A.
  How to write your own living will / by Edward A. Haman.-- 4th ed.
    p. cm.
  Includes index.
  ISBN 1-57248-394-6 (alk. paper)
  1. Right to die--Law and legislation--United States--States--Popular
works. I. Title.
KF3827.E87 H356 2004
344.7304'197--dc22
                                                2004024876

Printed and bound in the United States of America.

VHG — 10 9 8 7 6 5 4 3 2

CONTENTS

USING SELF-HELP LAW BOOKS

Before using a self-help law book, you should realize the advantages and disadvantages of doing your own legal work and understand the challenges and diligence that this requires.

The Growing Trend

Rest assured that you won't be the first or only person handling your own legal matter. For example, in some states, more than seventy-five percent of the people in divorces and other cases represent themselves. Because of the high cost of legal services, this is a major trend and many courts are struggling to make it easier for people to represent themselves. However, some courts are not happy with people who do not use attorneys and refuse to help them in any way. For some, the attitude is, "Go to the law library and figure it out for yourself."

We write and publish self-help law books to give people an alternative to the often complicated and confusing legal books found in most law libraries. We have made the explanations of the law as simple and easy to understand as possible. Of course, unlike an attorney advising an individual client, we cannot cover every conceivable possibility.

Cost/Value Analysis

Whenever you shop for a product or service, you are faced with various levels of quality and price. In deciding what product or service to buy, you make a cost/value analysis on the basis of your willingness to pay and the quality you desire.

When buying a car, you decide whether you want transportation, comfort, status, or sex appeal. Accordingly, you decide among such choices as a Neon, a Lincoln, a Rolls Royce, or a Porsche. Before making a decision, you usually weigh the merits of each option against the cost.

When you get a headache, you can take a pain reliever (such as aspirin) or visit a medical specialist for a neurological examination. Given this choice, most people, of course, take a pain reliever, since it costs only pennies; whereas a medical examination costs hundreds of dollars and takes a lot of time. This is usually a logical choice because it is rare to need anything more than a pain reliever for a headache. But in some cases, a headache may indicate a brain tumor and failing to see a specialist right away can result in complications. Should everyone with a headache go to a specialist? Of course not, but people treating their own illnesses must realize that they are betting on the basis of their cost/value analysis of the situation. They are taking the most logical option.

The same cost/value analysis must be made when deciding to do one's own legal work. Many legal situations are very straight forward, requiring a simple form and no complicated analysis. Anyone with a little intelligence and a book of instructions can handle the matter without outside help.

But there is always the chance that complications are involved that only an attorney would notice. To simplify the law into a book like this, several legal cases often must be condensed into a single sentence or paragraph. Otherwise, the book would be several hundred pages long and too complicated for most people. However, this simplification necessarily leaves out many details and nuances that would apply to special or unusual situations. Also, there are many ways to interpret most legal questions. Your case may come before a judge who disagrees with the analysis of our authors.

Therefore, in deciding to use a self-help law book and to do your own legal work, you must realize that you are making a cost/value analysis. You have decided that the money you will save in doing it yourself outweighs the chance that your case will not turn out to your satisfaction. Most people handling their own simple legal matters never have a problem, but occasionally people find that it ended up costing them more to have an attorney straighten out the situation than it would have if they had hired an attorney in the beginning. Keep this in mind while handling your case, and be sure to consult an attorney if you feel you might need further guidance.

Local Rules   The next thing to remember is that a book which covers the law for the entire nation, or even for an entire state, cannot possibly include every procedural difference of every jurisdiction. Whenever possible, we provide the exact form needed; however, in some areas, each county, or even each judge, may require unique forms and procedures. In our state books, our forms usually cover the majority of counties in the state, or provide examples of the type of form which will be required. In our national books, our forms are sometimes even more general in nature but are designed to give a good idea of the type of form that will be needed in most locations. Nonetheless, keep in mind that your state, county, or judge may have a requirement, or use a form, that is not included in this book.

You should not necessarily expect to be able to get all of the information and resources you need solely from within the pages of this book. This book will serve as your guide, giving you specific information whenever possible and helping you to find out what else you will need to know. This is just like if you decided to build your own backyard deck. You might purchase a book on how to build decks. However, such a book would not include the building codes and permit requirements of every city, town, county, and township in the nation; nor would it include the lumber, nails, saws, hammers, and other materials and tools you would need to actually build the deck. You would use the book as your guide, and then do some work and research involving such matters as whether you need a permit of some kind, what type and grade of wood are available in your area, whether to use hand tools or power tools, and how to use those tools.

Before using the forms in a book like this, you should check with your court clerk to see if there are any local rules of which you should be aware, or local forms you will need to use. Often, such forms will require the same information as the forms in the book but are merely laid out differently or use slightly different language. They will sometimes require additional information.

Changes in   Besides being subject to local rules and practices, the law is subject to change at
the Law   any time. The courts and the legislatures of all fifty states are constantly revising the laws. It is possible that while you are reading this book, some aspect of the law is being changed.

In most cases, the change will be of minimal significance. A form will be redesigned, additional information will be required, or a waiting period will be extended. As a result, you might need to revise a form, file an extra form, or wait out a longer time period; these types of changes will not usually affect the outcome of your case. On the other hand, sometimes a major part of the law is changed, the entire law in a particular area is rewritten, or a case that was the basis of a central legal point is overruled. In such instances, your entire ability to pursue your case may be impaired.

To help you with local requirements and changes in the law, be sure to read the section in Chapter 3 on "Legal Research."

Again, you should weigh the value of your case against the cost of an attorney and make a decision as to what you believe is in your best interest.

Introduction

This book is designed to enable you to prepare your own living will without hiring a lawyer. It will explain the law regarding living wills, guide you in deciding which form you need, and give you the information you need to prepare it. If you have not already done so, be sure to read the previous section on "Using Self-Help Law Books."

The difficulty in covering any area of law on a national scale is that the law is different in each state. However, the general type of information found in most living wills is very similar in all states. Appendix A of this book will give you some information about your state's specific laws. Many states have officially approved living will forms. These forms are found in Appendix C, along with general forms for use in any state that does not have its own form. In addition to living wills, this book will also discuss some related forms, such as the **HEALTH CARE POWER OF ATTORNEY** and **DO NOT RESUSCITATE ORDER.**

Before beginning to read Chapter 1, you may find it helpful to familiarize yourself with some terminology by reviewing the terms defined in the Glossary.

The old saying that "knowledge is power" is especially true in the law. This book will give you a fair amount of knowledge. By reading this book, you will know as much about living wills as some recent law school graduates.

Read this entire book (including the listing for your state in Appendix A) before you prepare any papers. This will give you the information you need to decide what form to use and how to complete it. You may also want to visit your local law library to get more information, or just to be sure the law has not changed since this book was published. The section on "Legal Research" in Chapter 3 will help you with further searches.

To complete the necessary form (or forms), you will need to use the general information in the main part of this book, consult the listing for your state in Appendix A, read any instructions on the form itself, and use the information from any additional reading and research. To help you with some legal terms, check the Glossary after Chapter 6.

I | LIVING WILLS AND RELATED DOCUMENTS

Thinking about why you might need a *living will* is not pleasant, but it is a matter that cannot be avoided. With advances in medical science, it is often possible to keep someone technically alive indefinitely. Instead of allowing terminally ill patients to die a natural death, many are kept alive by the use of drugs and machines. A situation can also arise where a person becomes permanently unconscious, but is not going to die as long as food and water are provided. Either condition can place a burden, both emotionally and financially, upon the person's loved ones.

Some people believe that all human life is sacred and that life should be preserved at all costs. Others believe that certain steps should be taken to preserve life, but some steps should not be taken. Regardless of the view you take, it may one day be important that your family members and doctors know your opinion. You can make your beliefs and desires known through a living will.

Living Wills

A *living will* is simply a paper on which you explain your desires in the event medical conditions arise that cause you not to be able to express your wishes. A living will is usually limited to the refusal of, or desire for, medical treatment in the event of:

- ✪ a terminal illness;

- ✪ an injury; or,

- ✪ permanent unconsciousness.

In the event you are unable to communicate your desires in such situations and do not have a living will, doctors or hospitals may decide they are legally obligated to perform certain procedures that you would not desire. If your spouse, adult child, or another relative is called upon to make a decision about your care, he or she will find it helpful if you have expressed your wishes in a living will. A living will tells others what you want to happen in such circumstances.

You may see a living will called by other names, such as:

- ✪ a declaration regarding life-prolonging procedures;

- ✪ an advance directive; or,

- ✪ a declaration.

Traditional Will Compared

A *traditional will* expresses what you want to happen to your property and minor children if you die. A *living will* expresses what you want to happen to your person regarding medical treatment while you are still alive.

Health Care Power of Attorney

In addition to a living will, you should also be aware of another type of document that can be of help in these difficult situations. That document is a *health care power of attorney*. A health care power of attorney gives someone you trust, usually a family member or close friend, the authority to make decisions about your medical treatment. You may also see this referred to as a *durable power of attorney for health care, health care proxy, designation of health care surrogate, advance health care directive*, or a similar name.

A health care power of attorney goes farther than a living will. A living will simply states—*If I am terminally ill or permanently unconscious and cannot tell my doctors what I want, then this is what I want done.* The big restriction with a living will is that it only applies if you are terminally ill or permanently unconscious. If you are only temporarily unconscious or otherwise unable to communicate, but are *not* terminally ill, a living will is of no use. You need a health care power of attorney to cover such a situation.

With a health care power of attorney, you give another person the power to make decisions about your medical treatment if you are unable to communicate, even if you are *not* terminally ill or permanently unconscious. This would include approving and giving consent to surgery or other treatment.

A living will may be used along with a health care power of attorney, and may even be included in the power of attorney, as a guide for the person making decisions on your behalf. Some of the official state forms accomplish this. Also, recent court cases, particularly one in Florida, demonstrate that it can be crucial to have both of these documents.

In that case, a young woman who suffered severe brain injury had neither a living will nor a health care power of attorney. Florida law allows certain family members to make health care decisions in the absence of these documents. When the husband sought to have a feeding tube removed, the woman's parents filed and lawsuit, followed by numerous appeals. When all of that failed, they sought the intervention of the state legislature and the governor to counteract the court decision.

As this book goes to press, the battle between the family members has been going on for over two year, and is continuing as the husband asks the courts to invalidate the actions of the legislature and governor. Even if this woman had a living will, it might still give room for argument between the parents and husband. If she also had a health care power of attorney designating her husband as her agent, her parents would likely have little room for argument. However, some people prefer a living will to a health care power of attorney because there is not anyone to whom they want to give that type of authority.

Living Will Choices

In its most basic form, a living will says—*If I become terminally ill or injured, I do not want any artificial means used that will only delay my death.* This is still the basic form used by many of the states that have created living will forms. Over the years, more issues have risen, resulting in slightly more complex forms being developed. These issues include:

✪ conditions of permanent unconsciousness, irreversible coma, or where death is not imminent;

✪ conditions where the burdens of treatment outweigh the expected benefits but death is not imminent;

✪ distinctions between various types of medical procedures;

✪ providing food and water through feeding tubes or intravenously;

✪ alternative provisions or exceptions if the person is pregnant;

✪ organ donations; and,

✪ covering the situation where a person *does* want all possible measures taken to preserve life.

Such provisions have been included in the forms approved by some states. These choices will be discussed more fully in later chapters.

Basic Documents for Your Protection

Having a living will is beneficial, but to be better protected, you would be well-advised to have all four of the following basic documents.

✪ A *living will,* which tells your health care providers, and your health care agent if you also have a health care power of attorney, what your wishes are if you become terminally ill or permanently unconscious.

✪   A *durable power of attorney for health care,* which gives a trusted relative or friend the power to make all types of health care decisions if you are unable to do so.

✪   A *durable financial power of attorney,* which gives a trusted relative or friend the ability to handle your financial matters if you become incapacitated.

> ***Warning:*** Great caution must be used here because the person you name as your agent could take your money and other property if he or she is dishonest.

✪   A *will,* which insures that your property goes to whom you wish to have it and provides for the care and custody of any minor children.

2 LAWYERS

The law regarding living wills is fairly simple. There are very few variables to living will forms. By the time you are finished reading this book, you will know as much as some lawyers do about how to prepare a living will.

The purpose of a living will is to express your desires. A living will needs to accurately reflect your wishes and meet certain legal requirements for it to be honored by health care providers (as is discussed in Chapter 3). Living will forms are often available from various senior citizen and other activist groups. However, these may not follow the form approved by the legislature of your state.

The way most lawyers would approach this is to first consult your state laws to see if there is an approved form. If not, he or she would possibly consult a book such as this one, look at examples of other living wills, and prepare a document to fit your situation. That is what this book will enable you to do for yourself.

If you decide to hire a lawyer, the remainder of this chapter will help you to select and work with him or her more effectively.

Selecting a Lawyer

Selecting a lawyer is a two-step process. First, you need to decide which attorney to make an appointment with; then you need to decide if you want to hire that attorney.

Finding Lawyers

Some suggestions to help you find a lawyer include the following.

- ✪ Ask a friend to recommend a lawyer he or she has hired and with whom he or she was happy.

- ✪ Use a lawyer referral service. You can find a lawyer by looking in the Yellow Pages phone directory under "Attorney Referral Services" or "Attorneys." This is a service, usually operated by a bar association, that is designed to match a client with an attorney handling cases in the area of law the client needs. The referral service does not guarantee the quality of work, the level of experience, or the ability of the attorney.

- ✪ Check under the heading for "Attorneys" in the Yellow Pages phone directory for display ads indicating attorneys' areas of practice.

- ✪ Ask another lawyer you know, or have used in the past for some other matter, if he or she handles living wills, or could refer you to an attorney who does.

Evaluating a Lawyer

You should select three to five lawyers worthy of further consideration from your search. Your first step will be to call each attorney's office, explain that you are interested in having a living will prepared, and ask the following questions.

- ✪ Does the attorney (or firm) handle preparation of a living will?

- ✪ How much can you expect it to cost?

- ✪ How soon can you get an appointment?

If you like the answers you receive, ask if you can speak to the attorney. Some offices will permit this, but others will require you to make an appointment. Make the appointment if required. Once you get in contact with the attorney (either on the phone or at the appointment), ask the following questions.

✪ How much will it cost, and how will the fee be paid?

✪ How long has the attorney been in practice?

✪ Has the attorney handled this type of matter before?

✪ How long will it take to get a document prepared?

If you get acceptable answers to these questions, it is time to ask *yourself* the following questions about the lawyer:

✪ Do you feel comfortable talking to the lawyer?

✪ Is the lawyer friendly toward you?

✪ Does the lawyer seem confident in him- or herself?

✪ Does the lawyer seem to be straight-forward with you and able to explain things so that you understand?

If you get satisfactory answers to all of these questions, you probably have a lawyer with whom you will be able to work. Most clients are happiest using an attorney with whom they feel comfortable.

Working with a Lawyer

In general, you will work best with your attorney if you keep an open, honest, and friendly attitude. There are also a few suggestions you could use to help the situation.

Ask Questions
If you want to know something or if you do not understand something, ask your attorney. If you do not understand the answer, tell your attorney and ask him or her to explain it again. You should not be embarrassed to ask questions. Many people who say they had a bad experience with a lawyer either did not ask enough questions or had a lawyer who would not take the time to explain things to them. If your lawyer is not taking the time to explain what he or she is doing, it may be time to look for a new lawyer.

Give Complete Information
Anything you tell your attorney is confidential. An attorney can lose his or her license to practice if he or she reveals information without your permission. So do not hold back information.

Accept Reality
Listen to what your lawyer tells you about the law and the legal system, and accept it. It will do you no good to argue because the law or the system does not work the way you think it should. Remember, it is not your attorney's fault that the system is not perfect or that the law does not say what you would like it to say.

Be Patient
Do not expect your lawyer to return your phone calls within an hour. He or she may not be able to return your calls the same day. Most lawyers are very busy and overworked. It is rare that an attorney can maintain a full caseload and still make each client feel as if he or she is the only client.

Talk to the Secretary
Your lawyer's secretary can be a valuable source of information. Be friendly to and get to know the secretary. He or she will often be able to answer your questions and you will not get a bill for the time.

Keep Your Case Moving
Many lawyers operate on the old principle of *the squeaking wheel gets the oil.* Work on a case tends to get put off until a deadline is near, an emergency develops, or the client calls. The reason for this is that many lawyers take more cases than can be effectively handled in order to earn the income they desire. Your task is to become a squeaking wheel that does not squeak so much that the lawyer wants to avoid you. Whenever you talk to your lawyer, ask the following questions:

- ✪ What is the next step?

- ✪ When do you expect it to be done?

- ✪ When should I talk to you next?

If you do not hear from the lawyer when you expect, call him or her the following day. Do not remind him or her of the missed phone call—just ask how things are going.

How to Save Money
One of the first concerns you may have about a lawyer is cost. For a very rough estimate, you can probably expect an attorney to charge anywhere from $75 to $300 per hour. Most will prepare a living will for a flat fee—probably between $20 and $75. If you and your spouse each want a living will, the cost will

double. A lawyer may then also suggest that you have a health care power of attorney and update your will, which could involve considerably higher costs.

Of course, you do not want to spend unnecessary money for an attorney. There are a few things you can do to avoid excess legal fees.

- ✪ Do not make unnecessary phone calls to your lawyer.

- ✪ Give information to the secretary whenever possible.

- ✪ Direct your question to the secretary first. He or she will refer it to the attorney if he or she cannot answer it.

- ✪ Plan your phone calls so you can get to the point and take less of your attorney's time. Write down an outline if necessary.

- ✪ Do some of the leg work yourself. For example, pick up and deliver papers yourself. Ask your attorney what you can do to assist.

- ✪ Be prepared for appointments. Have all related papers with you, plan your visit to get to the point, and make an outline of what you want to discuss and what questions you want to ask.

Pay Your Attorney Bill When It is Due   No client gets prompt attention like a client who pays on time. However, you are entitled to an itemized bill, showing what the attorney did and how much time it took. If your attorney asks for money in advance, you should be sure that you and the lawyer agree on what is to be done for the fee.

Firing Your Lawyer   If you find that you can no longer work with your lawyer or do not trust your lawyer, it is time to either prepare a living will alone or get a new attorney. You will need to send your lawyer a letter stating that you no longer desire his or her services and are discharging him or her from your case. Also state that you will be coming by his or her office the following day to pick up your file. The attorney does not have to give you his or her own notes or other work he or she has in progress, but he or she must give you the essential contents of your file (such as copies of papers already prepared and billed for and any documents you provided). If he or she refuses to give your file to you for any reason, contact your state's bar association about filing a complaint or *grievance* against the lawyer. Of course, you will need to settle any remaining fees owed.

3 | THE LAW CONCERNING LIVING WILLS

The basics of the law concerning living wills is fairly simple. By signing a living will, you are telling your family, friends, doctors, hospitals, and other health care providers what type of health care you want (or do not want) in certain situations.

The basic reason for having a living will is to get a third party, usually a doctor or hospital, to perform your wishes if you become terminally ill, injured, or permanently unconscious. The concern of the doctor is that he or she may be held liable, either civilly or criminally, for not performing a medical procedure that some could argue would have allowed you to live longer.

Many states have passed laws that allow a doctor to honor a living will without being subject to any liability.

These laws provide that other people may rely on your wishes as expressed in your living will and will not be legally responsible for honoring those wishes.

Example: You state in your living will that you do not want artificial life support procedures used if your condition is terminal. Your doctor will not be subject to a lawsuit by your estate or family for discontinuing life support procedures. Without a living will, the doctor or hospital may be reluctant to discontinue such artificial life support procedures.

In states that do not have such a law, it may be more difficult to get a doctor to follow your living will instructions. In such cases, it is important that you discuss your wishes with your spouse, family members, or friends, so that someone is fully aware of how you feel. They may then be willing to seek a court order to end artificial life support procedures and the living will can be used to convince the judge of your wishes.

Some states have laws that authorize certain family members to make these life and death health care decisions even without a living will. However, it will probably be easier for your family members to make such decisions if they are certain how you feel about the subject. A living will can clearly express your desires.

The Law in Your State

Many states have established approved forms for living wills. Some are separate living will forms and others are living will provisions within a health care power of attorney form. First, refer to the listing for your state in Appendix A. It will tell you about the living will laws in your state, which form to use, and where to locate your state's laws if you wish to do further reading. You can then locate the proper form in Appendix C and complete it. (State forms can vary in a few areas.)

Type of Conditions

There are several types of situations that may be covered in a living will. Some state forms refer to only one situation, while others include two or more. The following is a brief explanation of these situations, including where problems occur in the language of some state forms. Where necessary, these matters will be discussed in more detail in each state's listing in Appendix A.

Terminal conditions. In some states, *terminal conditions* may be called *terminal illness* or *terminal injury*, and may also be accompanied by further language in an attempt to clearly describe the situation. In many state forms, you will find language to the effect that the condition must be *incurable* or *irreversible*, or that death must be likely to occur *within a relatively short period of time*. In most cases, there is no definition of what constitutes *a relatively short period of time*, and in practice, this is left to the doctors to determine.

In a few states, the language of the form requires that it must be determined that the person will die *whether or not life-sustaining procedures are utilized.* One of the central purposes of a living will is to allow the person to die where life-sustaining procedures could keep him or her alive indefinitely. To require death to be imminent even if life-sustaining procedures are used defeats the whole purpose of the living will. This is probably just a case of poor drafting of the form. The intent of the legislature was probably to say, as the Texas form provides, that *death is imminent or will result within a relatively short time without the application of life-sustaining procedures.* In practice, the poor drafting of these forms will probably be overlooked, and the obvious intent will be recognized. However, if a doctor with a lawyer's mind, or an attorney for a hospital or the doctor, ever reads the state form carefully, problems may arise in getting your living will enforced.

It is still advisable to use the official form for your state, as it will probably be quickly recognized and followed by doctors and hospitals. To provide clarification of these poorly drafted forms, you may wish to use form 58 along with the official form for your state. Form 58 gives you options to select that may better explain your desires. This form also states that it is for the purpose of clarifying and detailing your desires and provides that if it, or any part of it, is determined to be legally invalid, the remainder of the living will remains in effect.

Permanent unconsciousness. A person in a coma who is not likely to recover consciousness is what generally describes *permanent unconsciousness.* This may also be called a persistent vegetative state, being permanently comatose, having permanent loss of the ability to communicate concerning medical treatment decisions, or similar language. In several state forms, the language appears to also require the person's condition to be terminal, while in other states, permanent unconsciousness is a sufficient basis on which to invoke the living will even if the person's condition is *not* terminal.

Where the burdens of treatment outweigh the benefits. Only a few states allow as a basis for invoking a living will a condition where the burdens of treatment outweigh the benefits. This basis does not require a terminal condition.

Oregon law. Two other situations for invoking a living will are available in Oregon. These are where the person has an *advanced progressive illness* (this is defined in the official state form) and where the use of life support would cause *permanent and severe pain* and would not help the person's condition.

As a practical matter, except for the Oregon provisions, the factors listed above will usually be connected with a very serious condition that will be either terminal or constitute permanent unconsciousness.

Food and Water   Some state forms have provisions relating to artificially provided food and water, commonly referred to as *nutrition and hydration*. Some forms are silent on this subject, some require it to be provided, others include it as part of the life-sustaining procedures that will be withheld or withdrawn, and others give various types of options to select. If your state's form does not include a provision about food and water or if you do not like the choices available in your state's form, you may want to complete form 58 (see p.225) and attach it to your state's form. Form 58 will give you more options in this area. (This subject is discussed in more detail in Chapter 4.)

Doctor Certification   A question may arise as to when a person meets the qualifications to invoke his or her living will.

> **Example:**   If a person must be either in a terminal condition or permanently unconscious, how is it determined whether he or she is in a terminal condition or permanently unconscious?

Some states are silent on this subject and others require one or more doctors to certify that the circumstances exist. See your state's listing in Appendix A for the certification requirements of your state. (This will be discussed more in Chapter 5.)

Witnesses and Notaries   States differ as to their requirements for how the living will must be signed. All states require the person making the living will to sign and date it. What differs is who must witness the person signing. Depending upon the state, the required witnesses may be: 1) two or more witnesses; 2) two witnesses and a notary public; or, 3) either two witnesses or a notary public. Where both witnesses and a notary are required, some states only require the maker's signature to be notarized, while others require notarization of the signatures of the maker and both witnesses.

Regardless of what may be required in your state, it is strongly suggested that you have two witnesses and that your signature and your witnesses signatures all be notarized. This may be an extra precaution if it is not legally required in your state, but it may make doctors and hospitals more likely to honor your living will without question. It may also be helpful in the event that your living will needs to be invoked while you are in another state. See your state's listing in Appendix A for the requirements of your particular state.

Pregnancy   Another issue may arise when a woman is pregnant and she develops a medical condition that would call for the implementation of her living will. Many state forms do not address this situation. Most states that do address this situation provide that the living will is temporarily invalid, or suspended, during the duration of the pregnancy. In such states, all efforts are made to keep the woman alive until the child can be born, regardless of the wishes of the person. The forms for Arizona and Maryland have optional provisions to cover pregnancy.

Other Variations   There are other various matters that may be covered in living will forms. These include:

- ✪ designating a person to see that your living will is honored;

- ✪ authorizing organ donation;

- ✪ expressing wishes regarding an autopsy;

- ✪ requesting that all efforts be made to preserve life;

- ✪ designating which procedures are, or are not, desired;

- ✪ specific revocation provisions;

- ✪ designating a primary physician; and,

- ✪ designating a guardian.

Where appropriate, such matters will be mentioned in the listing for your state in Appendix A or described in the form for your state in Appendix C.

Generally you should not need to go beyond the information in this book. However, if you wish to study your state's law on living wills or health care powers of attorney, the next section of this chapter will give you more information about using the law library and Internet sources.

Legal Research

After reading this book, you may want to visit your local law library to do some additional research. One can usually be found at your county courthouse or at a law school. Do not hesitate to ask the law librarian to help you find what you need. The librarian cannot give you legal advice, but can show you where to find your state's laws and other books on living wills.

Statutes or Code   The main source of information is the set of books containing your state's laws. These are the *statutes*, or *code*, of your state (e.g., *Florida Statutes*, *Mississippi Code*, etc.). The title of the books may also include words such as "Revised" or "Annotated" (e.g., *Annotated California Code*, *Kentucky Revised Statutes*, etc.). *Revised* means updated and *annotated* means the books contain information that explains and interprets the laws. Titles may also include the publisher's name, such as *Purdon's Pennsylvania Consolidated Statutes Annotated*. The listing in Appendix A gives the title of the set of laws for your state.

Each year, the legislatures in all states meet and change the law. Therefore, it is important to be sure you have the most current version. The most common way to update laws is with a soft-cover supplement, which found in the back of each volume. There will be a date on the cover to tell you when it was published. Laws can be updated in other ways, like:

✪   with a supplement volume, which is found at the end of the regular set of volumes;

✪   a looseleaf binding, in which pages are removed and replaced; or,

✪   a supplement section added as the law changes.

Checking the most current law is probably all you will need. The following sources may be helpful if you want to go further:

Internet Research. Another place to find statutes, as well as other legal materials, is on the Internet. The statutes or code for most states can be found on a state sponsored site on the Internet or at **www.findlaw.com**. Appendix B has instructions on finding the laws for each state.

Practice Manuals. A *practice manual* is a book or set of books containing detailed information about various areas of the law. They usually include forms for all different situations.

Digests. A *digest* is a set of books that gives summaries of appeals court cases. A digest for your state is best (such as *Florida Digest* or *Texas Digest*), as the national digest is difficult to use. Look in the index for the subject you want, such as "Living Wills," "Advance Directives," "Life-Prolonging Procedures," "Health Care Power of Attorney," etc.

Case Reporters. Sets of books called *case reporters*, or *reporters*, contain the full written opinions of the appeals court cases. The cases in the reporters are arranged according to dates they were decided, not according to subject matter. Therefore, you will need to use another source, such as a digest or a legal encyclopedia, to find relevant cases in the reporters.

Legal Encyclopedia. A *legal encyclopedia* is used just like a regular encyclopedia. Look up the subject you want (such as "Living Wills" or "Health Care Power of Attorney") in alphabetical order. *American Jurisprudence* and *Corpus Juris Secundum* are the names of the major sets. Some states have their own, such as *Florida Jurisprudence*.

4 | WRITING YOUR LIVING WILL

A *living will* is a written statement that expresses your wishes to others regarding the use of specifically defined *life-prolonging procedures* in the event you become terminally ill, injured, or permanently unconscious.

Living wills only relate to certain situations, usually where a person has an injury or illness that is fairly certain to result in death or where the person is in a persistent vegetative state. They typically provide that one or two doctors must determine that death is fairly certain or that the person is in a persistent vegetative state with no hope of recovery. Once this determination is made, the living will tells your family, doctors, hospitals, and other health care providers, and your health care agent if you have one, what types of medical procedures you do, or do not, want.

Living Wills and Specific Situations

Originally, living will forms were merely statements that a person did not want life-prolonging procedures if he or she became terminally ill or injured. All that was needed was for the person to fill in his or her name, sign, and date the form. Sometimes, they were also signed by witnesses, and sometimes they were notarized. Some of the forms approved by state legislatures are still of this simple nature.

Over the years it became apparent that often people were facing complicated situations, and forms were developed to cover a wider range of possibilities. Many forms now allow you to make choices on matters such as:

- ✪ including coverage for a persistent vegetative state, even if the person's condition is not terminal;

- ✪ specifying which medical procedures you do or do not want;

- ✪ determining the use of artificial nutrition and hydration (i.e., the use of gastric tubes and intravenous feeding);

- ✪ stating that you do want life-prolonging procedures; and,

- ✪ having spaces for you to write in any other specific instructions or wishes regarding your medical treatment.

Some forms approved by state legislatures have one or more of these features. If your state's form does not include a provision you would like, you can either write it in on the state form, attach a sheet of paper with the additional provision, use form 58 in Appendix C, or use the forms in this book as guides for preparing your own custom form. Just be sure to use the signature, witness, and notary formats found on the form for your state (or use form 57, p.224 if there is no form for your state).

Artificial Nutrition and Hydration

The most common question when these situations arise is whether to provide the person with food and water. If the person will quickly die without artificial means to maintain heart or lung function, then providing food and water will not be an issue. However, this may become important if the person is not likely to die or not likely to die soon.

Most people want to be as comfortable as possible, even if they want to be allowed to die. Withholding food or water can cause additional pain. Some people are willing to accept this pain in order to hasten death (and overall relief). Others would rather live a little longer if it means avoiding pain. You will find this option in many of the forms in Appendix C. To decide which option is best for you, it would be a good idea to discuss the matter with your doctor, a nurse, or some other health care professional.

Living Will Forms

Many states have adopted specific living will forms, which are usually very similar. The following states have such statutory forms.

- Alabama
- Alaska
- Arizona
- Arkansas
- California
- Colorado
- Connecticut
- Delaware
- Florida
- Georgia
- Hawaii
- Idaho
- Illinois
- Indiana
- Iowa
- Kansas
- Kentucky
- Louisiana
- Maine
- Maryland
- Minnesota
- Mississippi
- Missouri
- Montana
- Nebraska
- Nevada
- New Hampshire
- New Mexico
- North Carolina
- North Dakota
- Ohio
- Oklahoma
- Oregon
- Pennsylvania
- Rhode Island
- South Carolina
- South Dakota
- Tennessee
- Texas
- Utah
- Vermont
- Virginia
- Washington
- West Virginia
- Wisconsin
- Wyoming

Forms specific for these states are found in Appendix C. Many of these forms have instructions right on the form, so be sure to read through it carefully. If your state is not listed above, you may want to check the most current version of your state's statutes or code because your state legislature could adopt a form at any time. Some states have very simple living will forms, where all you need to do is fill in the date and sign the form before witnesses or a notary public. Other states have specific living will provisions within a statutory health care power of attorney form. Still others just have spaces for you to write in any wishes you may have regarding life-prolonging procedures.

For some states with no separate living will form, but with a living will provision within a power of attorney form, the entire state power of attorney/living will form has been included in Appendix C. If all you want is a living will, you can just complete the living will portions of the form and the section for signatures, witnesses, and notary.

If you live in one of the states listed on the previous page as having a living will form, refer to Appendix C for your particular state form. The state living will forms found in this appendix are basically as simple as form 1 (discussed below), so the instructions given below for form 1 will help you complete your state form. (As indicated, many state forms also have instructions on the forms themselves.) All of them are simple to complete.

For further help, see the sample completed form for Minnesota beginning on page 27 in this chapter. (The Minnesota form was selected because it is not a simple *check-the-box* form like those for most states, and it requires the most work to complete.)

Living Will   If you do not live in one of the states with its own living will form in
(form 1)   Appendix C, you may use form 1. Follow these instructions to complete the **LIVING WILL** (form 1):

◈   Type your name on the line in the first, unnumbered paragraph.

◈   Include your complete date of birth on the next line found in that paragraph.

◈   Read paragraphs 1, 2, and 3. Initial the line before the paragraph or paragraphs that agree with your wishes. Paragraph 1 concerns terminal illnesses or injuries. Paragraph 2 concerns irreversible coma, permanent unconsciousness, and persistent vegetative states. Paragraph 3 concerns the situation where the burdens of treatment outweigh the expected benefits.

◈   Initial paragraph 4 *only* if you *do want* life-prolonging procedures.

NOTE: *As to paragraphs 1 through 3, you may initial any one paragraph, two of these paragraphs, or all three of these paragraphs. If you initial any of these three paragraphs, do not initial paragraph 4. If you initial paragraph 4, do not initial any of the paragraphs 1 through 3.*

If you initial any of the paragraphs 1 through 3, you must also initial the line before all of the medical treatments listed that you do not want. For most people, this will probably be all of them.

There is also item "g" for you to indicate any other specific treatments you do not want that are not already listed.

◈ Paragraph 5 provides space to type in any special instructions. (You are not required to fill in anything here.)

◈ Fill in the date.

◈ Type in your address where indicated below the signature line.

◈ Take the form and your two witnesses to a notary public (you can probably find a notary at your bank). Sign your name on the signature line, before two witnesses and a notary public. Also have the two witnesses sign before the notary on the lines marked "Witness," and type in the witnesses' names and addresses below their signatures. (Not all states require a notary, but it will not hurt to have a notary attest to the signatures. This will also make the form appear more official to a doctor or hospital, and make them more likely to honor it.)

Witnesses

Many states prohibit certain people from serving as a witness to a living will. Some of the state forms spell out who may or may not serve as a witness, so be sure to read the form carefully. The list contained in this section covers most, if not all, of the types of persons who *may not* serve as a witness in at least one state. By avoiding the types of people listed, you will most likely avoid using an improper witness. However, to be certain of exactly who may or may not serve as a witness in your state, you should check the most current version of your state's laws.

Generally, it is *not* a good idea to have a witness who is:

✪ your spouse;

✪ your parent;

✪ your child;

✪ related to you by blood, adoption, or marriage;

✪ your physician or an employee of your physician;

✪ a provider of health care to you, or an employee, agent, or patient of such a health care provider;

NOTE: *This includes places such as hospitals and nursing homes, and their administrators, operators, and employees. It generally only applies to persons connected with a facility where you reside or which provides services to you.*

Example: If you have a friend who happens to work at a nursing home, but you are not a resident of that nursing home, that friend may act as your witness.

✪ entitled to any part of your estate, either by law or through your will or who has any kind of claim against your estate;

✪ a beneficiary on your life insurance policy;

✪ directly financially responsible for your medical care;

✪ under the age of eighteen; or,

✪ the person named as your agent in a health care power of attorney.

Notarized Signatures

Even if your state does not require a living will to be notarized, it is a good idea to have it notarized. This is just one more thing that may make it more likely for a health care provider to honor the living will without question. It will also be helpful if you are travelling to a state where living wills must be notarized.

Form 57 (see p. 224) is a notary page that you can attach to your living will (of course this is not necessary if you are in a state with an approved form that already has a notary provision).

NOTE: *Some states have specific requirements as to the form of a notarization statement (which can also be changed by the legislature at any time). Check with the notary you intend to use to be sure the notary format is valid for your state.*

HEALTH CARE LIVING WILL

Notice:

This is an important legal document. Before signing this document, you should know these important facts:

(a) This document gives your health care providers or your designated proxy the power and guidance to make health care decisions according to your wishes when you are in a terminal condition and cannot do so. This document may include what kind of treatment you want or do not want and under what circumstances you want these decisions to be made. You may state where you want or do not want to receive any treatment.

(b) If you name a proxy in this document and that person agrees to serve as your proxy, that person has a duty to act consistently with your wishes. If the proxy does not know your wishes, the proxy has the duty to act in your best interests. If you do not name a proxy, your health care providers have a duty to act consistently with your instructions or tell you that they are unwilling to do so.

(c) This document will remain valid and in effect until and unless you amend or revoke it. Review this document periodically to make sure it continues to reflect your preferences. You may amend or revoke the living will at any time by notifying your health care providers.

(d) Your named proxy has the same right as you have to examine your medical records and to consent to their disclosure for purposes related to your health care or insurance unless you limit this right in this document.

(e) If there is anything in this document that you do not understand, you should ask for professional help to have it explained to you.

TO MY FAMILY, DOCTORS, AND ALL THOSE CONCERNED WITH MY CARE:

I, ___Mary L. Jones___, born on ___April 1___, 19_48_ (birthdate), being an adult of sound mind, willfully and voluntarily make this statement as a directive to be followed if I am in a terminal condition and become unable to participate in decisions regarding my health care. I understand that my health care providers are legally bound to act consistently with my wishes, within the limits of reasonable medical practice and other applicable law. I also understand that I have the right to make medical and health care decisions for myself as long as I am able to do so and to revoke this living will at any time.

(1) The following are my feelings and wishes regarding my health care (you may state the circumstances under which this living will applies):
I do not want my life prolonged by life-sustaining treatment if it is determined by 2 physicians who have examined me that I have a terminal condition, or that I am in a permanently unconscious state.

(2) I particularly want to have all appropriate health care that will help in the following ways (you may give instructions for care you do want):
Any type of care or treatment that will provide me with comforts and alleviate pain, even if such care or treatment hastens my death.

(3) I particularly do not want the following (you may list specific treatment you do not want in certain circumstances):

<u>See paragraph (5) below.</u>

(4) I particularly want to have the following kinds of life-sustaining treatment if I am diagnosed to have a terminal condition (you may list the specific types of life-sustaining treatment that you do want if you have a terminal condition):

<u>None.</u>

(5) I particularly do not want the following kinds of life-sustaining treatment if I am diagnosed to have a terminal condition (you may list the specific types of life-sustaining treatment that you do not want if you have a terminal condition):

<u>Any type of life-sustaining treatment, including but not limited to, CPR, artificial breathing, kidney dialysis, drugs or antibiotics, surgery or other invasive procedures, or transfusions of blood or blood products.</u>

(6) I recognize that if I reject artificially administered sustenance, then I may die of dehydration or malnutrition rather than from my illness or injury. The following are my feelings and wishes regarding artificially administered sustenance should I have a terminal condition (you may indicate whether you wish to receive food and fluids given to you in some other way than be mouth if you have a terminal condition):

<u>I do not want artificially administered sustenance unless it is the opinion of my attending physician that withholding or withdrawing such sustenance would cause me undue pain that cannot be alleviated with medication.</u>

(7) Thoughts I feel are relevant to my instructions. (You may, but need not, give your religious beliefs, philosophy, or other personal values that you feel are important. You may also state preferences concerning the location of your care.):

(8) **Proxy Designation.** (If you wish, you may name someone to see that your wishes are carried out, but you do not have to do this. You may also name a proxy without including specific instructions regarding your care. If you name a proxy, you should discuss your wishes with that person.)

If I become unable to communicate my instructions, I designate the following person(s) to act on my behalf consistently with my instructions, if any, as stated in this document. Unless I write instructions that limit my proxy's authority, my proxy has full power and authority to make health care decisions for me. If a guardian or conservator of the person is to be appointed for me, I nominate my proxy named in this document to act as guardian or conservator of my person.

Name: Joseph P. Jones
Address: 123 Main Street, Minneapolis, MN 55401
Phone Number: 555-5155
Relationship: (If any) Husband

If the person I have named above refuses or is unable or unavailable to act on my behalf, or if I revoke that person's authority to act as my proxy, I authorize the following person to do so:

Name: Janet A. Smith
Address: 1431 Elm Street, St. Paul, MN 55101
Phone Number: 555-1155
Relationship: (If any) Sister

I understand that I have the right to revoke the appointment of the persons named above to act on my behalf at any time by communicating that decision to the proxy or my health care provider.

(9) **Organ Donation After Death.** (If you wish, you may indicate whether you want to be an organ donor upon your death.) Initial the statement which expresses your wish:

<u>M L J</u> In the event of my death, I would like to donate my organs. I understand that to become an organ donor, I must be declared brain dead. My organ function may be maintained artificially on a breathing machine, (i.e., artificial ventilation), so that my organs can be removed.

Limitations or special wishes: (If any) I would like to donate organs for any purpose, but I do not wish to donate my body for research or education purposes.

I understand that, upon my death, my next of kin may be asked permission for donation. Therefore, it is in my best interests to inform my next of kin about my decision ahead of time and ask them to honor my request.
I (~~have~~) (have not) agreed in another document or on another form to donate some or all of my organs when I die.

_____ I do not wish to become an organ donor upon my death.

DATE: April 21, 2004   SIGNED: *Mary L. Jones*

STATE OF Minnesota

COUNTY OF Hennepin

Subscribed, sworn to, and acknowledged before me by Mary L. Jones on this 21st day of April, 200 4 .

C. U. Sine
NOTARY PUBLIC

OR

(Sign and date here in the presence of two adult witnesses, neither of whom is entitled to any part of your estate under a will or by operation of law, and neither of whom is your proxy.)

I certify that the declarant voluntarily signed this living will in my presence and that the declarant is personally known to me. I am not named as a proxy by the living will, and to the best of my knowledge, I am not entitled to any part of the estate of the declarant under a will or by operation of law.

Witness _____   Address _____

_____

Witness _____   Address _____

_____

Reminder: *Keep the signed original with your personal papers. Give signed copies to your doctor, family, and proxy.*

USING YOUR LIVING WILL

Knowing what to do with a living will is just as important as having one.

Example 1: Betty reads a magazine article telling her she needs a living will. She has one prepared, stating that she does not want any artificial life-support provided if she is ever in a terminal condition, and signs it. Figuring that she should keep it with her other important papers, she puts it in her safe deposit box. She never mentions the living will to anyone. Eight months later, Betty is in a serious car accident. She is brought to the hospital unconscious and it quickly becomes obvious to the emergency room doctor that her injuries are so severe that she will never regain consciousness. She will die soon unless she is hooked up to machines to keep her heart and lungs working. Her living will clearly states that she does not want to be hooked up to the machines, but since her living will is locked up in her safe deposit box, no one is aware of her wishes. Betty is hooked up to the machines with the permission of her daughter.

Example 2: In a situation basically the same as above, except here Betty's living will states that she wants all efforts made to preserve her life. Betty lives in a state that allows a spouse or an adult child to make this type of decision for a person who cannot communicate his or her desires. Again, her living will is locked in her safe deposit box, and no one knows her wishes. Betty's daughter tells the doctor not to hook Betty to the machines, believing this to be what Betty would want.

Copies of Your Living Will

From the examples you can see it is important to let people know that you have a living will. For this reason, you should give copies to:

✪ your spouse, adult children, or other close relatives or friends who may be contacted in the event you suffer a terminal illness or injury;

✪ your regular, primary care doctor;

✪ any specialist physician who is treating you;

✪ the local hospital where you are likely to be taken in an emergency;

✪ any hospital, outpatient surgery center, or other health care facility where you will be receiving treatment;

✪ any person you may have named as your agent in a health care power of attorney; and,

✪ any nursing home or other type of assisted living facility in which you reside. (This may also be required by state law.)

NOTE: *Carry a copy of your living will with you whenever you travel.*

Living Wills and Emergency Medical Care

There have been a few horror stories of an emergency medical technician (EMT) refusing to provide emergency care to a person once it is learned the person has a living will. An EMT has no business making a decision as to whether a person is in a terminal condition, permanently unconscious, or in any other state that would bring a living will into effect. Such determinations need to be made by a physician.

For purposes of emergency medical services, it is not necessary for the technician to know if the patient has a living will. If you are ever asked by an EMT if you have a living will, the safest response may be *No*. If asked if another person has a living will, the safest response may be *Not that I know of.* (This should not be confused with a *do not resuscitate order*, which is briefly discussed in Chapter 6.)

6 OTHER HEALTH CARE FORMS

In addition to a living will, many other health care forms exist and should be part of your overall consideration. These additional forms include:

- ✪ health care power of attorney;

- ✪ directives for specific medical procedures;

- ✪ do not resuscitate orders;

- ✪ revocation of living will; and,

- ✪ statement of desires and location of property and documents.

This chapter discusses these forms and explains when and how to use them.

Health Care Power of Attorney

The *health care power of attorney* was discussed briefly in Chapter 1. This is a document in which you designate someone to be your representative in the event you are unable to make or communicate decisions about all aspects of your health care. In the most basic form, a health care power of attorney merely says, *I want this person to make decisions about my health care if I am unable to do so.* The more recent trend is to either have a separate living will to give your agent some guidance, or to incorporate living will provisions in the health care power of attorney. A health care power of attorney can be as broad as possible, or can limit the type of decisions the person can make. If you do not have a living will, or do not make any type of statements in your health care power of attorney about you desires, it will be up to the person you designate to determine what you would want in a certain situation. It can be a great help to your agent if you also have a living will or living will provisions in the power of attorney to provide some guidance as to what you would like.

Some of the official state forms have a provision where you can designate someone to carry out your wishes, or to make all health care decisions on your behalf. Particularly as a result of the fiasco in Florida discussed in Chapter 1, it is becoming apparent that a health care power of attorney is as valuable as a living will. If your state's form does not have such a provision, a **DURABLE POWER OF ATTORNEY FOR HEALTH CARE** (form 59, p.227) has been included in Appendix C. Of course, keep in mind that you should only use a health care power of attorney if there is someone whom you trust to make health care decisions on your behalf.

Directives for Specific Medical Procedures

A living will is generally executed well in advance of the need for medical procedures. However, when someone knows he or she will be going in the hospital for surgery, a specific form can be signed just for that particular hospital stay. Such a form can be more detailed and specific than a living will. Many hospitals have such forms for patients to complete prior to the procedure.

"Do Not Resuscitate" Orders

A *do not resuscitate order* is a written order of a physician informing health care providers that no resuscitation efforts are to be made in the event the patient's heart or breathing stops. This type of order may be abbreviated *DNR*, and is also sometimes called a *no code* order.

Traditionally, a DNR order was issued by the attending physician when he or she believed that resuscitating the patient would do nothing but delay death and prolong pain. A DNR order was typically just a notation in the patient's medical record or was a simple form posted near the patient's bed. This was often done without the knowledge of the patient or the patient's family members. More recently, some states have passed laws giving family members rights to make decisions about DNR orders and to allow a person to make an advance directive for a DNR order that is applicable to emergency medical technicians (EMTs).

NOTE: *This is different from an EMT refusing to treat because of the existence of a living will.*

Such laws are currently on the books in Alaska, Arizona, Arkansas, Colorado, Connecticut, Idaho, Maryland, Montana, New York, Rhode Island, South Carolina, Tennessee, Utah, Virginia, and West Virginia.

Revoking a Living Will

If you execute a living will, then change your mind, there are two things you can do. First, you can execute a new living will that expresses your current desires. This has the effect of cancelling your previous living will. Second, you can simply revoke your living will without making a new one.

Revocation of Living Will (form 2) Most state laws provide that you may revoke your living will by simply telling your doctor. However, to be certain your doctor understands that you have changed your mind, it would be better to put your revocation in writing. To do this, use the **REVOCATION OF LIVING WILL** (form 2, p.98).

To complete form 2:

◈ Type in your name and address on the first line in the main paragraph.

◈ Type in the title of the living will you are revoking on the second line. This will be the title as it appears on the document, such as "Living Will," "Declaration," "Advance Directive," etc.

➔ Type in the date of the living will you are revoking on the third line.

➔ Type in the date on the line indicated, and sign on the signature line (sign before a notary if the living will you are revoking was also signed before a notary).

The form for Missouri (form 27, p.153) contains a revocation provision. If you live in Missouri, you do not need to use form 2 to revoke your **DECLARATION,** but can complete the revocation provision on form 27.

Statement of Desires

In addition to a living will and a traditional will, you may want to have another document informing your family of certain things that you wish to have done. This can be accomplished with a **STATEMENT OF DESIRES AND LOCATION OF PROPERTY & DOCUMENTS** (form 56, p.221). This is not a legally binding document, but merely a statement of your wishes that you hope your family will follow.

In the event of death, many people have certain desires regarding the type of funeral and burial (or cremation, etc.) and other matters that cannot be taken care of in a will. A will may not be discovered until after burial, so it would do no good to include funeral and burial instructions in your will.

Another thing that can be done with such a document is to give your family members important information that will assist them in taking care of your estate. The following matters may be included:

✪ location of your will;

✪ a list of your assets;

NOTE: *It is not always easy for the person handling your estate to find everything that you own, especially things like stocks, bonds, and similar investments. Things stored somewhere other than at your home such as a coin collection in a safe deposit box, a boat at a docking facility, a recreational vehicle in a storage lot, furniture at a self-storage company, etc., are often difficult to locate. Your list should include a detailed description of the item and where it is located.*

✪ a list of your life insurance policies, including the name, address, and telephone number of the insurance company (and of your insurance agent), and the policy number;

✪ a list of relatives, friends, and any other people you would like to be notified of your death. (Include their names, addresses, and telephone numbers.);

✪ any desires you may have regarding the education and upbringing of your minor children;

✪ provisions for the custody and care of pets. (You do not want your pets to go unfed while you are in the hospital, so be sure you discuss pet care with the relative or friend who will be notified in the event of an emergency. Your will should also state who you want to have your pets, and possibly include giving money to that person for food, veterinary care, etc.); and,

✪ instructions regarding your funeral. (This should include information about any cemetery plot you may own, any prepaid funeral plan, whether you want a traditional burial, burial at sea, cremation, etc., as well as any personal desires such as the type of music you want played. You may specify a lavish funeral or state that you wish the least expensive burial in order to save assets for your heirs.)

In order for such a document to be of any use, it must be in a place where it can easily be found by a family member. Therefore, it is not a good idea to put it in your safe deposit box. Once the bank finds out about your death, it may seal your safe deposit box and only permit it to be opened with a court order. Because it takes time to obtain a court order, it may be well after the funeral that the contents of the safe deposit box become available.

GLOSSARY

It is helpful to know some commonly used terms in order to understand living wills. The definitions in this glossary are not technical legal definitions, since the words and phrases may be defined differently in various states or not defined at all. Nor are they technical medical definitions. Rather, they are general definitions to help you understand the ideas they express, regardless of how they may be specifically defined legally or medically.

A

agent. A person who is given authority to act on behalf of another by a power of attorney.

artificial hydration. The use of feeding tubes (either through the mouth, nose, or intravenously) to provide water (hydration) to a person who is unable to drink in a normal manner.

artificial nutrition. The use of feeding tubes (either through the mouth, nose, or intravenously) to provide food (nutrition) to a person who is unable to eat in a normal manner.

attorney-at-law. A person licensed to practice law before state or federal courts. The term has no relationship to a *power of attorney* or an *attorney-in-fact*.

attorney-in-fact. The person given authority by a power of attorney. This is another term for agent that is used in many statutes. An attorney-in-fact does not have the power to represent anyone in court or to give legal advice.

D

declarant. A person who signs a living will, usually when the living will document is titled "Declaration."

do not resuscitate order (DNR). A physician's written instruction that a patient not be resuscitated in the event the patient's heart stops beating or in the event breathing stops.

durable power of attorney. This is a power of attorney that continues to be effective after the principal becomes incapacitated.

E

execute. To sign a legal document in the legally required manner, thereby making it valid and effective.

H

health care power of attorney. A specific type of power of attorney that gives your agent (usually a family member or close friend) the authority to make decisions about your medical treatment. You may also see this referred to as a *durable power of attorney for health care, health care proxy, designation of health care surrogate, advance health care directive,* or some similar name.

L

living will. A document that states what treatment a person does or does not desire in certain circumstances.

life-prolonging procedures. Medical procedures applied to a person with a terminal illness or injury in order to delay death. Examples are machines used to maintain respiration and blood circulation. These are sometimes also referred to as *life sustaining procedures.*

N

no code order. *See do not resuscitate order.*

P

persistent vegetative state. This is the term frequently used to describe the situation where a person is unconscious or in a coma, and has virtually no hope of regaining consciousness. It may also be referred to by other terms, such as *permanently unconscious* or *permanently comatose.*

power of attorney. A document that gives one person (the agent or attorney-in-fact) authority to act on behalf of another person (the *principal*). Traditionally, a power of attorney related to financial matters, but now there are also health care powers of attorney.

principal. This is another name for the person who signs a *living will* or *power of attorney.*

proxy. Another term for agent.

S

surrogate. Another term for the agent in a *health care power of attorney.*

T

terminal illness, injury, or condition. An illness or injury that is extremely likely to result in death. Some states require that death is likely to occur *within a relatively short time,* but do not say what constitutes a relatively short time.

W

will. A will expresses what you want to happen to your property (and any minor children) if you die. It should not be confused with a *living will,* which expresses what medical treatment you want (or do not want) while you are still alive.

APPENDIX A: STATE LAWS

This appendix lists each state alphabetically and gives information about each state's laws concerning living wills. The following subjects are summarized for the applicable states.

THE LAW: This tells you where to find the law on living wills for your state. It will give the full title of the set of law books, with an example of how it is abbreviated. The symbol "§" means "section." Ask the librarian if you have any difficulty finding the set of books containing the laws for your state. (In this section, it will also be noted if the state has any provisions for health care powers of attorney, although such forms are beyond the scope of this book.)

FORM(S): This tells you which form you will need from Appendix C. First find the title of the form, followed by the form number. If your state has not adopted an official form, the **LIVING WILL** (form 1) is listed. If your state has adopted an official form, the name and number of that form is given.

You will also find a notation for optional forms. These are forms you may want to use in addition to form 1 or the official form for your state. In all states, the **STATEMENT OF DESIRES AND LOCATION OF PROPERTY & DOCUMENTS** (form 56) is listed as an optional form. (See page 38 for more information on form 56.) If your state's form does not have a provision for a notary public, form 57 will be listed as an optional form. (See page 26 for more information about signing before a notary public.) If your state's living will form is so basic that it may not clearly state your desires, form 58 will be listed as an optional form. Form 58 is basically the same as form 1. Use the instructions for form 1 on page 24 to help you complete form 58.

TYPES OF CONDITIONS: This tells you the various circumstances covered by the state's form. For the exact language and definition of terms, see your state's statutes or code. Words in quotation marks are direct quotes from either the state's form or the state's statute or code section. The most common types of situations covered by living wills follow.

✪   *Terminal conditions.* This is an illness or injury that is fairly certain to result in death. Many of the forms require death to be likely to occur "within a relatively short time," or some similar language. In most states, it is not certain what is meant by a relatively short time.

✪   *Persistent vegetative state.* This may also be referred to as *permanently unconscious, permanently comatose, in a coma,* etc. The idea is that the person is not aware of his or her surroundings, not able to communicate, and the condition is unlikely to change (the person's condition need not be terminal).

✪   *Where the burdens of treatment outweigh the benefits.* This is where treatment will cause pain or discomfort, without appreciable benefits for the person or improvement of the condition (the person's condition need not be terminal).

DOCTOR CERTIFICATION: This tells you if there are any requirements for one or more physicians to officially certify the existence of the condition required for the living will to take effect. In some states, the person's doctor makes this determination informally. In other states, the physician must verify the condition in writing (usually by making a notation in the patient's medical record). In still other states there must be a written certification by two physicians. Occasionally, the number or types of physicians certifying depends upon the nature of the condition being verified. (For example, only one physician needs to certify to a terminal condition, but two must certify to permanent unconsciousness.)

FOOD & WATER: This tells you whether the state's form has any provisions regarding providing food and water to a patient by artificial means (i.e., by feeding tube through the mouth, nose, or intravenously). Some forms include this as a treatment to be withheld or withdrawn, others allow the person to choose whether this is to be included, and other forms do not say anything at all about this subject.

WITNESSES: This tells you how many people need to witness your signature, and whether the signing needs to be notarized. As mentioned earlier in this book, it is a good idea to have signatures notarized, even if your state does not require it. (see Chapter 4.)

MISCELLANEOUS: This gives any information that does not relate to one of the other categories. Most frequently noted will be optional provisions in the form and whether the form includes a pregnancy exception. In some states, a living will may not be enforced if the person is pregnant. In such states, treatment is given to keep the person alive until the child can be born. Once the child is delivered, the living will goes back into effect and further treatment can be stopped. These notes will mention where possible problems may arise.

ALABAMA

THE LAW:	"Natural Death Act," Code of Alabama, Title 22, Chapter 8A, Section 22-8A-1 (C.A. § 22-8A-1). Form at C.A. § 22-8A-4 allows you to designate a person to serve as your *proxy* for assuring that your living will is carried out. You may also find the Code in a set of books titled "*Michie's* Alabama Code."
FORM(S):	**ADVANCE DIRECTIVE FOR HEALTH CARE** (form 3); includes provision for acceptance by the proxy, which is required. Optional: forms 56 and 57.
TYPES OF CONDITIONS:	Applies to terminal condition and permanent unconsciousness.
DOCTOR CERTIFICATION:	Two physicians, one of whom is the attending physician.
FOOD & WATER:	May not be withheld or withdrawn unless specified in the living will.
WITNESSES:	Two witnesses; no notary.
MISCELLANEOUS:	Form has pregnancy exception.

ALASKA

THE LAW:	Alaska Statutes, Title 18, Chapter 12, Section 18.12.010 (A.S. § 18.12.010), titled "Living Wills and Do Not Resuscitate Orders." Form at A.S. § 18.12.010(c). DNR: A.S. § 18.12.035.
FORM(S):	**DECLARATION** (form 4). Includes provision for organ donation. Optional: forms 56 and 58.

TYPES OF CONDITIONS:	Applies to an "incurable or irreversible condition" that will cause death "within a relatively short time."
DOCTOR CERTIFICATION:	Attending physician must certify to a "terminal condition" in person's medical record.
FOOD & WATER:	Has optional provision.
WITNESSES:	If signed by another person at the direction of the declarant, must have two witnesses OR notary.
MISCELLANEOUS:	Cards, necklaces, bracelets, etc., identifying a person as having a living will or do not resuscitate order are available from the Department of Health and Social Services.

ARIZONA

THE LAW:	Arizona Revised Statutes, Section 36-3261 (A.R.S. § 36-3261). Form at A.R.S. § 36-3262. (There is also a "Prehospital Medical Care Directive," which is basically a DNR signed by the patient, A.R.S. § 36-3251.) For health care powers of attorney, see A.R.S. § 36-3224. For mental health power of attorney, see A.R.S. § 36-3286.
FORM(S):	**LIVING WILL** (form 5). Optional: form 56.
TYPES OF CONDITIONS:	Has options to cover terminal condition or irreversible coma and persistent vegetative state that doctor believes to be irreversible or incurable.
DOCTOR CERTIFICATION:	Not required.
FOOD & WATER:	Has optional provision.
WITNESSES:	One witness OR notary. Form 5 has space for two witnesses, which are recommended. If there

is only one witness, that person may not be related to the principal by blood, marriage, or adoption and may not be entitled to any part of the principal's estate by law or under a will at the time the living will is executed. No witness or notary may be designated to make medical decisions for the principal nor be directly involved in providing health care to the principal at the time the living will is executed.

MISCELLANEOUS: Form has optional pregnancy exception provision.

ARKANSAS

THE LAW: "Arkansas Rights of the Terminally Ill or Permanently Unconscious Act," Arkansas Code of 1987 Annotated, Title 20, Chapter 17, Section 20-17-201 (A.C.A. § 20-17-201). Form at A.C.A. § 20-17-202. DNR: A.C.A. § 20-13-901 to 908.

FORM(S): **DECLARATION** (form 6). In both main paragraphs, you must cross out one of the two statements in brackets "[ ]," whichever does **not** express your wishes. One is a statement that you want treatment withheld or withdrawn; the other appoints a person (called a *health care proxy*) to provide instructions. If you cross out the first option, you will need to fill in the name of the person you want as your health care proxy. Optional: forms 56 and 57.

TYPES OF CONDITIONS: Applies to an "incurable or irreversible condition" that will cause death "within a relatively short time," and to being "permanently unconscious."

DOCTOR CERTIFICATION: Attending physician and another physician must determine the conditions are met and attending physician must record it in the patient's medical record.

FOOD & WATER:	No provision.
WITNESSES:	Two witnesses; no notary.

CALIFORNIA

THE LAW:	Authorization for advance health care directive found at *West's* Annotated California Codes, Probate Code, Sections 4605 and 4673 (Probate Code §§ 4605 and 4673), with optional form provided at Section 4701. (Health care power of attorney provisions found at Probate Code, § 4700 et seq., titled "Durable Power of Attorney for Health Care." Health care power of attorney form found at A.C.C. § 4771.
FORM(S):	**ADVANCE HEALTH CARE DIRECTIVE** (form 7). Optional: form 56.
TYPES OF CONDITIONS:	Applies if there is an "incurable and irreversible condition that will result in death in a relatively short time" or "burdens of treatment" outweigh expected benefits.
DOCTOR CERTIFICATION:	Not required.
FOOD & WATER:	No provision.
WITNESSES:	Two witnesses, one must swear that he or she is not related to the individual or entitled to any part of the individual's estate; special witness requirement if a patient is in a skillled nursing facility; no notary.

COLORADO

THE LAW:	"Colorado Medical Treatment Decisions Act," *West's* Colorado Revised Statutes Annotated, Title 15, Article 18, Section 15-18-101 (C.R.S.A. § 15-18-101). Form at C.R.S.A.

§ 15-18-104. DNR: C.R.S.A. § 15-18.6-101 to 108 (called "CPR directive").

FORM(S):

DECLARATION AS TO MEDICAL OR SURGICAL TREATMENT (form 8). Optional: form 56.

TYPES OF CONDITIONS:

Applies if there is a terminal condition that is incurable or irreversible; or if "unconscious, comatose, or otherwise incompetent so as to be unable to make or communicate responsible decisions" for seven or more days. As written, it does not appear that a terminal condition is required to qualify under the provision for being unconscious, comatose, or incompetent for at least seven days.

DOCTOR CERTIFICATION:

Two physicians must certify to the condition being terminal, but not to being unconscious, comatose, or otherwise incompetent.

FOOD & WATER:

Has various options.

WITNESSES:

Two witnesses AND notary for signer and witnesses. Witnesses may not be anyone who is a patient in the same facility as the declarant, the declarant's attending physician or an employee of the attending physician, an employee of a health care facility treating the declarant, a person with a claim against the declarant's estate, or a person entitled to a portion of the declarant's estate by law or under a will at the time the living will is executed.

CONNECTICUT

THE LAW:

Connecticut General Statutes Annotated, Title 19a, Section 19a-570 (C.G.S.A. § 19a-570), titled "Removal of Life Support Systems." Form at C.G.S.A. § 19a-575. DNR: C.G.S.A. § 19a-580d. (Health care power of attorney form at C.G.S.A. §§ 19a-575a and 19a-577.)

FORM(S):	**DOCUMENT CONCERNING WITHHOLDING OR WITHDRAWAL OF LIFE SUPPORT SYSTEMS** (form 9). Optional: forms 56 and 57.
TYPES OF CONDITIONS:	Applies to terminal condition or if "permanently unconscious."
DOCTOR CERTIFICATION:	Not required.
FOOD & WATER:	Optional provisions (included as being withdrawn or withheld unless you cross it out and initial it).
WITNESSES:	Two witnesses; no notary.
MISCELLANEOUS:	Pregnancy exception in statute.

DELAWARE

THE LAW:	Delaware Code Annotated, Title 16, Section 2501 (D.C.A. 16 § 2501), titled "Health-Care Decisions." Living will form is Part 2 of the statutory health care power of attorney at D.C.A. § 2505.
FORM(S):	**ADVANCE HEALTH-CARE DIRECTIVE** (form 10). This form also includes provisions for a health care power of attorney, anatomical gifts, and designating a primary physician. Part 2 is the living will portion of this form. If you only want a living will, then only complete Part 2 and the signature/witness/notary sections. Optional: forms 56 and 57.
TYPES OF CONDITIONS:	Applies to terminal conditions and when a person is considered "permanently unconscious."
DOCTOR CERTIFICATION:	Not required.
FOOD & WATER:	Optional provisions.
WITNESSES:	Two witnesses; no notary.

DISTRICT OF COLUMBIA

THE LAW:

No specific provisions for living wills. (Health care power of attorney provisions found in District of Columbia Code, Title 21, Section 2201 (D.C.C. § 21-2201), titled "Health-Care Decisions." The books have "D.C. Code" on the spine and "District of Columbia Code" on the front cover. Health care power of attorney form at D.C.C. § 21-2207.)

FORM(S):

LIVING WILL (form 1). Optional: form 56.

FLORIDA

THE LAW:

Florida Statutes, Chapter 765, Section 765.301 (F.S. § 765.301). Living will form at F.S. § 765.303. (A health care power of attorney form called "Health Care Surrogate" may be found at F.S. § 765.203.) The law also contains provisions for family members to make health care decisions in the absence of a living will or health care power of attorney, F.S. § 765.401.

FORM(S):

LIVING WILL (form 11). **DESIGNATION OF HEALTH CARE SURROGATE** (form 12). Optional: forms 56, 57, and 58.

TYPES OF CONDITIONS:

Applies to a terminal condition with "no medical probability" of recovery, an end-stage condition, or a persistent vegetative state.

DOCTOR CERTIFICATION:

The "attending or treating" physician and one other.

FOOD & WATER:

No provision.

WITNESSES:

Two witnesses; no notary.

MISCELLANEOUS: Has space to designate a *surrogate* to carry out desires as expressed (*i.e.*, give consent to terminate or withhold treatment).

GEORGIA

THE LAW: Official Code of Georgia Annotated, Title 31, Chapter 32, Section 31-32-1 (O.C.G.A. § 31-32-1), titled "Living Wills." Living will form found at O.C.G.A. § 31-32-3. (Health care power of attorney provisions found in the "Durable Power of Attorney for Health Care Act," O.C.G.A. § 31-36-1. Health care power of attorney form at O.C.G.A. § 31-36-10.)

FORM(S):   **LIVING WILL** (form 13). Optional: forms 56 and 57.

TYPES OF CONDITIONS: Applies to terminal condition, a coma, or a persistent vegetative state.

DOCTOR CERTIFICATION: Attending physician must note condition in medical record.

FOOD & WATER: Has optional provisions.

WITNESSES: Two witnesses; no notary.

MISCELLANEOUS: Form has pregnancy exception that can be negated only if fetus is not viable and you initial the line in paragraph 5.

HAWAII

THE LAW: Hawaii Revised Statutes, Section 327E-1 (H.R.S. § 327E-1), titled "Uniform Health-Care Decisions Act (Modified)." Living will is part of health care power of attorney form found at H.R.S. § 327E-16. A physician's form for certifying disability may be found at H.R.S. § 327D-10.

FORM(S):	**ADVANCE HEALTH-CARE DIRECTIVE** (form 14). Optional: form 56.
TYPES OF CONDITIONS:	Applies to a terminal condition or the "permanent loss of the ability to communicate concerning medical treatment decisions."
DOCTOR CERTIFICATION:	Not required.
FOOD & WATER:	Has optional provisions.
WITNESSES:	Two witnesses OR notary.

IDAHO

THE LAW:	"Natural Death Act," Idaho Code, Title 39, Chapter 45, Section 39-4501 (I.C. § 39-4501). Living will form at I.C. § 39-4504. DNR: I.C. §§ 39-151 to 165.
FORM(S):	**A LIVING WILL** (form 15). Optional: forms 56 and 57.
TYPES OF CONDITIONS:	Applies to a terminal condition or being in a "persistent vegetative state."
DOCTOR CERTIFICATION:	Two "medical doctors."
FOOD & WATER:	Has optional provisions.
WITNESSES:	Two witnesses; no notary.
MISCELLANEOUS:	Has space to designate proxy to make health care decisions, but this paragraph also states "I have duly executed a Durable Power of Attorney for health care decisions on this date." Form has pregnancy exception.

ILLINOIS

THE LAW:	"Illinois Living Will Act," *West's* Smith Hurd Illinois Compiled Statutes Annotated, Chapter 755, Section 35/1 (755 ILCS 35/1). Form found at 755 ILCS 35/3. (Health care power of attorney covered in 755 ILCS 45/4-1. Health care power of attorney form at 755 ILCS 45/4-10. Also see "Health Care Surrogate Act," 755 ILCS 40/1.)
FORM(S):	**DECLARATION** (form 16). Optional: forms 56, 57, and 58.
TYPES OF CONDITIONS:	Applies to terminal conditions.
DOCTOR CERTIFICATION:	Not required.
FOOD & WATER:	No provisions.
WITNESSES:	Two witnesses; no notary.

INDIANA

THE LAW:	*West's* Annotated Indiana Code, Title 16, Article 36, Chapter 4, Section 16-36-4-1 (A.I.C. § 16-36-4-1). Indiana has one form for refusing (A.I.C. § 16-36-4-10) and one for requesting (A.I.C. § 16-36-4-11) life-prolonging procedures. (Information about health care powers of attorney found at A.I.C. § 16-36-1-1, but no form is provided. General power of attorney form under A.I.C. § 30-5-5-1, includes a provision for health care powers.)
FORM(S):	**LIVING WILL DECLARATION** (form 17), if you do ***not*** want life-prolonging procedures. Optional: forms 56, 57, and 58. **LIFE PROLONGING PROCEDURES DECLARATION** (form 18) if you ***do want*** life-prolonging procedures. Optional: forms 56 and 57.

TYPES OF CONDITIONS:	Form for refusing treatment applies to a terminal condition where "death will occur within a short time."
DOCTOR CERTIFICATION:	Refusal of treatment requires certification by the attending physician.
FOOD & WATER:	Refusal of treatment still requires the provision of food and water (*i.e.*, there is no option on the form to refuse food and water).
WITNESSES:	Two witnesses; no notary.

IOWA

THE LAW:	"Life-sustaining Procedures Act," Iowa Code Annotated, Section 144A.1 (I.C.A. § 144A.1); form at I.C.A. § 144A.3. (Health care power of attorney form at I.C.A. § 144B.5.)
FORM(S):	**LIVING WILL** (form 19). Optional: forms 56, 57, and 58.
TYPES OF CONDITIONS:	Applies to terminal condition and declarant not able to make treatment decisions.
DOCTOR CERTIFICATION:	Attending physician and one other physician must agree the condition is terminal. Attending physician must note in medical record.
FOOD & WATER:	No provisions.
WITNESSES:	Two witnesses OR notary.

KANSAS

THE LAW:	Kansas Statutes Annotated, Section 65-28,101 (K.S.A. § 65-28,101). Living will form found at K.S.A. § 65-28,103. (Health care power of attorney provisions found at K.S.A. § 58-625.

Health care power of attorney form found at K.S.A. § 58-632.) You may find these volumes as either *Vernon's* Kansas Statutes Annotated or Kansas Statutes Annotated, Official. The supplement is a pocket part in *Vernon's* and a separate soft-cover volume in the *Official*. Both sets have very poor indexes.

FORM(S): **DECLARATION** (Form 20).

KENTUCKY

THE LAW: "Kentucky Living Will Directive Act," Kentucky Revised Statutes, Chapter 311, Section 311.620 (K.R.S. § 311.620). Form at K.R.S. § 311.625. Look for volume 12.

FORM(S): **LIVING WILL DIRECTIVE** (form 21.) Optional: form 56.

TYPES OF CONDITIONS: Applies to terminal condition or if "permanently unconscious."

DOCTOR CERTIFICATION: Not required.

FOOD & WATER: Optional provisions.

WITNESSES: Two witnesses OR notary.

MISCELLANEOUS: Form has pregnancy exception.

LOUISIANA

THE LAW: "Natural Death Act," *West's* Louisiana Statutes Annotated, Revised Statutes, Section 40.1299.58.1 (LSA Rev. Stat. § 40:1299.58.1). Living will form at LSA Rev. Stat. § 40:1299.58.3. The set is divided into topics, such as "Civil Code," "Revised Statutes," etc. Be sure you have the volumes titled "*West's* LSA

Revised Statutes" on the spine, and "*West's Louisiana Revised Statutes*" on the front cover. You may also designate a living will on your Louisiana driver's license according to LSA Revised Statutes § 32:410.

FORM(S):

DECLARATION (form 22). Optional: forms 56, 57, and 58.

TYPES OF CONDITIONS:

This statutory form is confusing. In an apparent attempt to make it comprehensive, the legislature has drafted a document that contains so much verbiage that it isn't clear what it means. Many questions arise. For example, does the comatose state need to be accompanied by a terminal condition? If so, why even mention comatose states? Or, the form also states that death must "occur whether or not life-sustaining procedures are utilized." This goes against a central purpose of a living will, which is to avoid situations where life is maintained indefinitely by life-sustaining procedures.

DOCTOR CERTIFICATION:

Certification required by two physicians, one of whom is the attending physician.

FOOD & WATER:

No provision.

WITNESSES:

Two witnesses; no notary.

MAINE

THE LAW:

Living will is part of a health care power of attorney under the "Uniform Health-Care Decisions Act," Maine Revised Statutes Annotated, Title 18-A, Section 5-801 (18-A M.R.S.A. § 5-801). Form at 18-A M.R.S.A. § 5-804.

FORM(S):

ADVANCE HEALTH-CARE DIRECTIVE (form 23). You will note that this is a form that also includes provisions for a health care power of attorney, organ donation, and designating a primary physician. This form also has an optional provision for a pregnancy exception. Part 2 is the living will portion of this form. If you only want a living will, then only complete Part 2 and the signature/witness/notary sections. Optional: forms 56 and 57.

TYPES OF CONDITIONS: Applies to: (1) an incurable and irreversible condition that will result in death within a relatively short time; (2) unconsciousness with a reasonable degree of medical certainty that consciousness will not be regained; and, (3) where the likely risks and burdens of treatment outweigh the expected benefits.

DOCTOR CERTIFICATION: Not required.

FOOD & WATER: Optional provisions.

WITNESSES: Two witnesses; no notary.

MARYLAND

THE LAW: Annotated Code of Maryland, Health-General, Section 5-601 (A.C.M., HG § 5-601). Living will and health care power of attorney forms at A.C.M., HG § 5-603. These volumes are arranged by subject, so be sure you have the volume marked "Health-General." Advance directive for DNR: A.C.M., HG § 5-608.

FORM(S):   **HEALTH CARE DECISION MAKING FORMS** (form 24). Optional: forms 56 and 57.

TYPES OF CONDITIONS: Applies in the case of a terminal condition and a persistent vegetative state with no expectation of recovery "within a medically appropriate period."

DOCTOR CERTIFICATION: Not required.

FOOD & WATER:	Optional provisions.
WITNESSES:	Two witnesses; no notary.
MISCELLANEOUS:	Space is provided to fill in any instructions to be followed in the event of pregnancy.

MASSACHUSETTS

THE LAW:	No specific provisions for living wills. (Health care power of attorney is discussed in Annotated Laws of Massachusetts, Chapter 201D, Section 1 (A.L.M., C. 201D, § 1).)
FORM(S):	**LIVING WILL** (form 1). Optional: form 56.

MICHIGAN

THE LAW:	No specific provisions for living wills. The index listing for "living wills" refers you to the provisions titled "Designation of patient advocate," which authorizes such a designation, but does not provide a form for either a living will or a health care power of attorney. Michigan Compiled Laws Annotated, Section 700.5506 (M.C.L.A. § 700.5506).
FORM(S):	**LIVING WILL** (form 1). Optional: form 56.
WITNESSES:	Two witnesses; no notary.

MINNESOTA

THE LAW:	"Minnesota Living Will Act," Minnesota Statutes Annotated, Section 145B.01 (M.S.A. § 145B.01). Living will form at M.S.A. § 145B.04. Living will can also be noted on a driver's license, M.S.A. § 171.07. (Health care power of attorney found at M.S.A. § 145C.01,

titled "Durable Power of Attorney for Health Care," form at M.S.A. § 145C.05.)

FORM(S):	**HEALTH CARE LIVING WILL** (form 25). This is not a *check-the-box* type of form or one that takes a certain position on various issues. You will need to fill in your wishes for each numbered paragraph. These include topics such as treatment options, food and water, organ donation, and designating a proxy and an alternate proxy. See pages 27 through 30 for a sample completed Minnesota form. Optional: form 56.

TYPES OF CONDITIONS:	Applies to a terminal condition, but also has a space to fill in specific circumstances.

DOCTOR CERTIFICATION:	Not required.

FOOD & WATER:	Optional provisions.

WITNESSES:	Notary OR two witnesses.

MISSISSIPPI

THE LAW:	"Uniform Health-Care Decisions Act," Mississippi Code 1972 Annotated, Title 41, Section 41-41-201 (M.C. § 41-41-201). Advance Health-Care Directive form, which includes sections for health care power of attorney, living will, and designation of primary physician, is found at M.C. § 41-41-209.

FORM(S):	**ADVANCE HEALTH-CARE DIRECTIVE** (form 26). Optional: form 56.

TYPES OF CONDITIONS:	Applies to: (1) a terminal condition; (2) permanent unconsciousness; or, (3) where "the risks and burdens of treatment would outweigh the expected benefits."

DOCTOR CERTIFICATION:	One physician.

FOOD & WATER:	Optional provision.
WITNESSES:	Two witnesses OR notary.

MISSOURI

THE LAW:	*Vernon's* Annotated Missouri Statutes, Chapter 459, Section 459.010 (A.M.S. § 459.010). Living will form at A.M.S. § 459.015. (Health care powers of attorney provided for in the "Durable Power of Attorney for Health Care Act," A.M.S. § 404.800. No health care power of attorney form provided.)
FORM(S):	**DECLARATION** (form 27). Optional: forms 56, 57, and 58.
TYPES OF CONDITIONS:	Applies to terminal conditions.
DOCTOR CERTIFICATION:	Not required.
FOOD & WATER:	No provision.
WITNESSES:	Two witnesses; no notary.
MISCELLANEOUS:	Form has revocation provision.

MONTANA

THE LAW:	"Montana Rights of the Terminally Ill Act," Montana Code Annotated, Title 50, Chapter 9, Section 50-9-101 (M.C.A. § 50-9-101). Form at M.C.A. § 59-9-103. DNR: M.C.A. § 50-10-101 to 107. The Montana Code is in paperback volumes, with the annotations in a separate set of binders.
FORM(S):	**DIRECTIVE TO PHYSICIANS** (form 28). Optional: forms 56, 57, and 58.

TYPES OF CONDITIONS:	Applies to an "incurable or irreversible condition" that will cause death "within a relatively short time."
DOCTOR CERTIFICATION:	Not required, however the form does state that it is to be the attending physician's opinion that the conditions are met.
FOOD & WATER:	No provision.
WITNESSES:	Two witnesses; no notary.

NEBRASKA

THE LAW:	"Rights of the Terminally Ill Act," Revised Statutes of Nebraska, Chapter 20, Section 20-401 (R.S.A. § 20-401). Living will form at R.S.N. § 20-404. (Heath care power of attorney provided for in R.S.N. § 30-3401, titled "Power of Attorney for Health Care," with form at R.S.N. § 30-3408.)
FORM(S):	**DECLARATION** (form 30). **POWER OF ATTORNEY FOR HEALTH CARE** (form 31). Optional: forms 56, 57, and 58.
TYPES OF CONDITIONS:	Applies to terminal condition or "persistent vegetative state."
DOCTOR CERTIFICATION:	Not required.
FOOD & WATER:	No provision.
WITNESSES:	Two witnesses OR notary.

NEVADA

THE LAW:	"Uniform Act on Rights of the Terminally Ill," Nevada Revised Statutes Annotated, Chapter 449, Section 449:535 (N.R.S.A. § 449:535).

Form for living will at N.R.S.A. § 449.610. (Health care power of attorney form at N.R.S.A. § 449.613, but it only gives authority for living will-type decisions, not for all types of health care decisions. Also see N.R.S.A. § 449.830.)

FORM(S):	**DECLARATION** (form 32). Optional: forms 56, 57, and 58.
TYPES OF CONDITIONS:	Applies to: (1) irreversible coma; (2) incurable or terminal condition or illness, with no reasonable hope of long term recovery or survival; or, (3) the burdens of treatment outweigh the expected benefits.
DOCTOR CERTIFICATION:	By attending physician in patient's medical record.
FOOD & WATER:	Optional provision.
WITNESSES:	Two witnesses OR notary. One of the witnesses must sign in two places.

NEW HAMPSHIRE

THE LAW:	New Hampshire Revised Statutes Annotated 1992, Chapter 137-H, Section 137-H:1 (N.H.R.S.A. § 137-H:1). Ignore "title" numbers; look for "chapter" numbers. Living will form at N.H.R.S.A. § 137-H:3. (Health care powers of attorney covered at N.H.R.S.A. § 137-J:1, with form at N.H.R.S.A. § 137-J:15.)
FORM(S):	**DECLARATION** (form 33). Optional: form 56.
TYPES OF CONDITIONS:	Applies to a "terminal" or "permanently unconscious" condition.
DOCTOR CERTIFICATION:	Two physicians.

FOOD & WATER:	Optional provision.
WITNESSES:	Two witnesses AND notary of signer and witnesses.

NEW JERSEY

THE LAW:	"New Jersey Advance Directives for Health Care Act," NJSA (for New Jersey Statutes Annotated), Title 26, Section 26:2H-53. The law authorizes both a "proxy directive" and an "instructional directive," but does not provide any forms.
FORM(S):	**LIVING WILL** (form 1). Optional: form 56.
TYPES OF CONDITIONS:	Applies to a "terminal" or "permanently unconscious" condition.
DOCTOR CERTIFICATION:	Attending physician and another must certify person lacks decision making capacity and so note in medical record. If incapacity is due to a mental or psychological condition, "a physician with appropriate special training or experience" must certify.
FOOD & WATER:	Included in the definition of "life-sustaining treatment."
WITNESSES:	Two witnesses who must attest that the declarant is of sound mind and free of duress or undue influence OR signature before notary, attorney at law, or other person authorized to administer oaths.
MISCELLANEOUS:	Statute provides that a living will can be supplemented with an audio or video tape recording. Statute provides that a woman may include any desired instructions in the event of pregnancy.

NEW MEXICO

THE LAW:	New Mexico Statutes 1978 Annotated, Chapter 24, Section 24-7A-1 (N.M.S.A. § 24-7A-1), titled "Uniform Health-Care Decisions." Living will is Part 2 of the health care power of attorney form and is titled "Instructions for Health Care." Health care power of attorney form at N.M.S.A. § 24-7A-4. A supplement to the Statutes is found at the end of each chapter.
FORM(S):	**OPTIONAL ADVANCE HEALTH-CARE DIRECTIVE** (form 34). You will note that this is a form that also includes provisions for a health care power of attorney and designating a primary physician. Part 2 is the living will portion of this form. If you only want a living will, only complete Part 2 and the signature/witness/notary sections. Optional: forms 56 and 57.
TYPES OF CONDITIONS:	Applies to: (1) terminal condition; (2) being permanently unconscious; and, (3) where "the likely risks and burdens of treatment would outweigh the expected benefits."
DOCTOR CERTIFICATION:	The "physician in charge" and one other physician must certify in writing to the terminal condition or irreversible coma, with a copy placed in the person's medical record.
FOOD & WATER:	Optional provisions.
WITNESSES:	Statute states it must be executed in the same manner as a will, but the official form just requires signature (and has spaces for two witnesses designated as "Optional").
MISCELLANEOUS:	Has optional provision to request all possible procedures.

NEW YORK

THE LAW:

No specific provisions for living wills. (*McKinney's* Consolidated Laws of New York Annotated, Public Health § 2980 (C.L.N.Y., Public Health § 2980), called "Health Care Agents and Proxies," relates to health care powers of attorney with form called "Health Care Proxy" found at § 2981(d).) Advance directive for DNR: C.L.N.Y., Public Health § 2960. This set of books is divided according to subject, so be sure you have the volume marked "Public Health."

FORM(S):

LIVING WILL (form 1). Optional: form 56.

NORTH CAROLINA

THE LAW:

Living will provisions at General Statutes of North Carolina, Chapter 90, Section 90-320 (G.S.N.C. § 90-320), titled "Right to Natural Death; Brain Death." Living will form at G.S.N.C. § 90-321(d). (Health care power of attorney at G.S.N.C. § 32A-15, titled "Health Care Powers of Attorney." Form at G.S.N.C. § 32A-25.) The North Carolina Secretary of State maintains an "Advance Health Care Directive Registry" where living wills can be registered.

FORM(S):

DECLARATION OF A DESIRE FOR A NATURAL DEATH (form 35). Optional: form 56.

TYPES OF CONDITIONS:

Applies to terminal condition or if "in a persistent vegetative state."

DOCTOR CERTIFICATION:

By attending physician and one other physician.

FOOD & WATER:

Optional provisions.

| WITNESSES: | Two witnesses AND acknowledgment of notary, court clerk, or assistant court clerk of signatures of the signer and witnesses. |

NORTH DAKOTA

THE LAW:	"Uniform Rights of Terminally Ill Act," North Dakota Century Code Annotated, Title 23, Chapter 23-06.4, Section 23-06.4-01 (N.D.C.C. § 23-06.4-01). Form at N.D.C.C. § 23-06.4-03. (Health care power of attorney found at N.D.C.C. § 23-06.5-1, titled "Durable Power of Attorney for Health Care." Health care power of attorney form at N.D.C.C. § 23-06.5-17.)
FORM(S):	**DECLARATION** (form 36). Optional: forms 56 and 57.
TYPES OF CONDITIONS:	Applies to terminal condition.
DOCTOR CERTIFICATION:	Two physicians.
FOOD & WATER:	Optional provisions.
WITNESSES:	Two witnesses; no notary.
MISCELLANEOUS:	Form has pregnancy exception.

OHIO

| THE LAW: | "Modified Uniform Rights of the Terminally Ill Act," *Page's* Ohio Revised Code Annotated, Section 2133.01 (O.R.S. § 2133.01) authorizes living wills (referred to as a "declaration" regarding "life-sustaining treatment") and gives some guidelines, but no statutory form is provided. This is a lengthy chapter of the Ohio Revised Code, placing all kinds of obligations and burdens on the physician, and includes matters such as procedures to be followed if a family member objects |

to terminating treatment. (Health care power of attorney at *Page's* Ohio Revised Code Annotated, Section 1337.11 (O.R.S. § 1337.11, but no form is provided. Also see O.R.S. § 2133.01, titled "Modified Uniform Rights of the Terminally Ill Act.") DNR: See O.R.S. § 2133.21.

FORM(S):   **DECLARATION** (form 37). Optional: form 56.

TYPES OF CONDITIONS: Applies to terminal condition or a "permanently unconscious state." The definition of these terms must be on the declaration in all capital letters.

DOCTOR CERTIFICATION: Attending physician and one other physician must certify that the person is terminally ill or in a permanently unconscious state; but only the attending physician must certify the person is unable to make an informed decision regarding the administration of life-sustaining treatment. These certifications must be noted in the patient's medical record.

FOOD & WATER: Optional provisions.

WITNESSES: Two witnesses OR notary. Witnesses or notary must attest that the declarant "appears to be of sound mind and not under or subject to duress, fraud, or undue influence."

MISCELLANEOUS: May include list of people to be notified by the attending physician if the living will is to be invoked. May include specific instructions regarding CPR.

OKLAHOMA

THE LAW: Living will is part of health care power of attorney form. Oklahoma Statutes Annotated, Title 63, Section 3101 (63 O.S.A. § 3101), titled "Oklahoma Rights of the Terminally Ill or Persistently Unconscious Act." Form at 63 O.S.A. § 3101.4.

FORM(S):	**ADVANCE DIRECTIVE FOR HEALTH CARE** (form 38). This form also includes provisions for a health care power of attorney (*proxy*) and anatomical gifts. Part I is the living will portion of this form. If you only want a living will, then only complete Part I and the signature and witness sections. Optional: forms 56 and 57.
TYPES OF CONDITIONS:	Applies to a terminal condition (must be determined that death will result within six months) or when the person is persistently unconscious.
DOCTOR CERTIFICATION:	Two physicians.
FOOD & WATER:	Optional provision.
WITNESSES:	Two witnesses; no notary.
MISCELLANEOUS:	Form has pregnancy exception.

OREGON

THE LAW:	Living will is a part of the health care power of attorney form. Oregon Revised Statutes Annotated, Chapter 127, Section 127.505 (O.R.S. § 127.505). The required health care power of attorney form found at O.R.S. § 127.531.
FORM(S):	**ADVANCE DIRECTIVE** (form 39). You will note that this is a form that also includes provisions for a health care power of attorney (*health care representative*). If you only want a living will, then only complete Part C and the signature/witness/notary sections. Optional: forms 56, 57, and 58.
TYPES OF CONDITIONS:	Applies if the person: (1) is close to death and life support would only postpone the moment of death; (2) is permanently unconscious; or, (3) has an advanced progressive illness (as described

in the form), or (4) if life support would cause "permanent and severe pain" and would not help the person's condition.

DOCTOR CERTIFICATION: Not required.

FOOD & WATER: Optional provisions.

WITNESSES: Two witnesses; no notary.

MISCELLANEOUS: Of special and unique interest is the Oregon Death With Dignity Act, O.R.S. § 127.800. This act allows a resident of Oregon to make a written "request for medication for the purpose of ending his or her life in a humane and dignified manner." The form is provided at O.R.S. § 127.897.

PENNSYLVANIA

THE LAW: "Advance Directive for Health Care Act," *Purdon's* Pennsylvania Consolidated Statutes Annotated, Title 20, Section 20-5401 (20 Pa.C.S.A. § 5401). Form is found at 20 Pa.C.S.A. § 5404.

FORM(S): **DECLARATION** (form 40). Optional: forms 56 and 57.

TYPES OF CONDITIONS: Applies if the person is in a terminal condition or a "state of permanent unconsciousness."

DOCTOR CERTIFICATION: Attending physician.

FOOD & WATER: Optional provision.

WITNESSES: Two witnesses; no notary.

MISCELLANEOUS: Pregnancy exception, unless: (1) the woman won't be maintained so as to permit the growth and birth of the child; (2) it would be physically harmful to the woman; or, (3) it would cause pain that can't be alleviated by medication.

RHODE ISLAND

THE LAW:

"Rights of the Terminally Ill Act," General Laws of Rhode Island, Section 23-4.11-1 (G.L.R.I. § 23-4.11-1). ("Health Care Power of Attorney Act" may be found beginning at G.L.R.I. § 23-4.10-1. Required health care power of attorney form at G.I.R.I. § 23-4.10-2.) DNR: G.L.R.I. § 23-4.11-14. Ignore "Title" and "Chapter" numbers.

FORM(S):

DECLARATION (form 41). **STATUTORY DURABLE POWER OF ATTORNEY FOR HEALTH CARE** (form 42).

TYPES OF CONDITIONS:

Applies if the person has an "incurable or irreversible condition" that will cause death "within a relatively short time."

DOCTOR CERTIFICATION:

Not required.

FOOD & WATER:

Optional provision.

WITNESSES:

Two witnesses; no notary.

SOUTH CAROLINA

THE LAW:

"Death With Dignity Act," Code of Laws of South Carolina, Title 44, Section 44-77-10 (C.L.S.C. § 44-77-10). (Health care power of attorney form at § 44-77-50. "Adult Health Care Consent Act" at C.L.S.C. § 44-66-10, discusses consent for medical treatment and states that this subject can be included in a durable power of attorney, but no form is provided.) DNR: C.L.S.C. § 44-78-10 to 65.

FORM(S):

DECLARATION OF A DESIRE FOR A NATURAL DEATH (form 43). The form states several optional revocation procedures. Also includes option to appoint an agent for the purpose of enforcing or revoking the living will. Optional: form 56.

TYPES OF CONDITIONS: Applies to terminal conditions or permanent unconsciousness. The determination of permanent unconsciousness may only be made after ninety consecutive days of unconsciousness.

DOCTOR CERTIFICATION: Two physicians.

FOOD & WATER: Optional provisions.

WITNESSES: Two witnesses AND notary of signer and witnesses.

SOUTH DAKOTA

THE LAW: South Dakota Codified Laws, Title 34, Section 34-12D-1 (S.D.C.L § 34-12D-1), titled "Living Wills." (Health care provisions are also authorized by S.D.C.L. §§ 59-7-2.5 and 34-12C-3, but no forms.)

FORM(S): **LIVING WILL DECLARATION** (form 44). Optional: forms 56 and 58.

TYPES OF CONDITIONS: Applies to terminal conditions.

DOCTOR CERTIFICATION: Not required.

FOOD & WATER: Optional provisions.

WITNESSES: Two witnesses; no notary required—however, the statutory form has space for notary to verify signature of signer and witnesses.

TENNESSEE

THE LAW:	"Tennessee Right to Natural Death Act," Tennessee Code Annotated, Title 32, Section 32-11-101 (T.C.A. § 32-11-101). Form at T.C.A. § 32-11-105. DNR: T.C.A. § 68-140-601.
FORM(S):	**LIVING WILL** (form 45). Optional: form 56.
TYPES OF CONDITIONS:	Applies to terminal conditions.
DOCTOR CERTIFICATION:	Not required.
FOOD & WATER:	Optional provisions.
WITNESSES:	Two witnesses; no notary required; however, the statutory form has space for notary to verify signature of signer and witnesses.
MISCELLANEOUS:	Also has option for organ donations.

TEXAS

THE LAW:	"Advance Directives Act," *Vernon's* Texas Codes Annotated, Health and Safety Code, Section 166.001 (T.C.A., Health and Safety Code § 166.001). Living will form at T.C.A., Health and Safety Code, § 166.033. [Medical Power of Attorney form at T.C.A., Health and Safety Code §§ 166.163 and 166.164.] The T.C.A. is divided into subjects, so be sure you have the proper subject volume. Also, be sure you have the volumes marked "*Vernon's* Texas Codes Annotated," not those marked "*Vernon's* Texas Civil Statutes," which have a volume marked "Health." DNR: T.C.A., Health and Safety Code § 166.081.

FORM(S):	**DIRECTIVE TO PHYSICIANS AND FAMILY OR SURROGATES** (form 46) and **MEDICAL POWER OF ATTORNEY** (form 47). Optional: Forms 56, 57, and 58.
TYPES OF CONDITIONS:	Applies to terminal conditions and irreversible conditions.
DOCTOR CERTIFICATION:	Two physicians must certify condition is terminal and attending physician must determine "death is imminent or will result within a relatively short time without the application of life-sustaining procedures."
FOOD & WATER:	No provision.
WITNESSES:	Two witnesses; no notary.
MISCELLANEOUS:	Form has pregnancy exception.

UTAH

THE LAW:	"Personal Choice and Living Will Act," Utah Code Annotated 1953, Title 75, Chapter 2, Section 75-2-1101 (U.C.A. § 75-2-1101). Form at U.C.A. § 75-2-1104. DNR: U.C.A. § 75-2-1105.5.
FORM(S):	**DIRECTIVE TO PHYSICIANS AND PROVIDERS OF MEDICAL SERVICES** (form 48). Optional: forms 56, 57, and 58.
TYPES OF CONDITIONS:	Applies to terminal condition or persistent vegetative state.
DOCTOR CERTIFICATION:	Two physicians.

FOOD & WATER: Provides that food and water *will* be withheld (the only way to designate otherwise is to cross out this provision).

WITNESSES: Two witnesses; no notary.

VERMONT

THE LAW: Vermont Statutes Annotated, Title 18, Section 5252 (18 V.S.A. § 5252). Ignore "Chapter" numbers. Living will is referred to as a "Terminal Care Document." Form at 18 V.S.A. § 5253. (Health care power of attorney is discussed at 14 V.S.A. §§ 3451 and 3452.)

FORM(S):   **TERMINAL CARE DOCUMENT** (form 49). Optional: forms 56, 57, and 58.

TYPES OF CONDITIONS: Applies to "terminal state."

DOCTOR CERTIFICATION: Not required.

FOOD & WATER: No provision.

WITNESSES: Two witnesses; no notary.

VIRGINIA

THE LAW: Living will is part of health care power of attorney (called an "Advance Medical Directive"), under the "Health Care Decision Act," Code of Virginia 1950, Title 54.1, Section 54.1-2981 (C.V. § 54.1-2981). Form at C.V. § 54.1-2984. DNR: C.V. § 54.1-2987.1. Ignore "Chapter" numbers and look for "Title" and "Section" numbers.

FORM(S):   **ADVANCE MEDICAL DIRECTIVE** (form 50). Has option to appoint health care agent. Optional: forms 56, 57, and 58.

TYPES OF CONDITIONS:	Applies to terminal conditions.
DOCTOR CERTIFICATION:	(1) Attending physician must determine the condition is terminal. (2) If a health care agent has been appointed, there must be written verification that the person is unable to make informed decisions by the attending physician and either another physician or a licensed clinical psychologist.
FOOD & WATER:	No provision.
WITNESSES:	Two witnesses; no notary.
MISCELLANEOUS:	Living will directive can be made orally before the attending physician and two witnesses.

WASHINGTON

THE LAW:	"Natural Death Act," *West's* Revised Code of Washington Annotated, Title 70, Chapter 122, Section 70.122.010 (R.C.W.A. § 70.122.010). Form called "Health Care Directive" is found at R.C.W.A. § 70.122.030. (Health care power of attorney is authorized by R.C.W.A. §§ 11.94.010 and 11.94.046, but no form is provided.)
FORM(S):	**HEALTH CARE DIRECTIVE** (form 51). Optional: forms 56 and 57.
TYPES OF CONDITIONS:	Applies to terminal or permanent unconscious conditions (these are further defined in the form).
DOCTOR CERTIFICATION:	The attending physician must certify a terminal condition; two physicians must certify to permanent unconsciousness.
FOOD & WATER:	Optional provision.

WITNESSES:	Two witnesses; no notary.
MISCELLANEOUS:	Form has pregnancy exception.

WEST VIRGINIA

THE LAW:	"West Virginia Natural Death Act," West Virginia Code, Chapter 16, Article 30, Section 16-30-1 (W.V.C. § 16-30-1). Living will and health care power of attorney forms found at W.V.C. § 16-30-4. DNR: "Do Not Resuscitate Act," W.V.C. § 16-30C-1; form at W.V.C. § 16-30C-6.
FORM(S):	**LIVING WILL** (form 52). **MEDICAL POWER OF ATTORNEY** (form 53). Optional: forms 56 and 58.
TYPES OF CONDITIONS:	Applies to terminal condition or persistent vegetative state.
DOCTOR CERTIFICATION:	Two physicians, one of whom is attending physician.
FOOD & WATER:	No provision. However, you can insert your own provision in the paragraph for listing any special directives or limitations.
WITNESSES:	Two witnesses AND notary of signer and witnesses.

WISCONSIN

THE LAW:	*West's* Wisconsin Statutes Annotated, Section 154.01 (W.S.A. § 154.01). Ignore "Chapter" numbers. Health care power of attorney authorized by W.S.A. § 155.01, but no form provided.
FORM(S):	**DECLARATION TO PHYSICIANS** (form 54). Optional: forms 56 and 57.
TYPES OF CONDITIONS:	Applies to terminal condition and persistent vegetative state.

| DOCTOR CERTIFICATION: | Two physicians. |

| FOOD & WATER: | Optional provisions. |

| WITNESSES: | Two witnesses; no notary. |

| MISCELLANEOUS: | Form has pregnancy exception. |

WYOMING

THE LAW: Wyoming Statutes Annotated, Title 35, Chapter 22, Section 35-22-101 (W.S.A. § 35-22-101), titled "Living Will." Living will form is found at W.S.A. § 35-22-102. (Health care power of attorney covered at W.S.A. § 3-5-201, titled "Durable Power of Attorney for Health Care," but no form provided.)

FORM(S): **DECLARATION** (form 55). Has space to designate someone to make treatment decisions for you. Optional: forms 56, 57, and 58.

TYPES OF CONDITIONS: Applies to terminal conditions where "death will occur whether or not life-sustaining procedures are utilized." If you think this is confusing, you are right. Here is a prime example of a legislature trying to be so comprehensive in explaining something, that it makes the law unclear. As written, this form fails to accomplish a central purpose of having a living will, which is to cover the situation where a person can be kept alive indefinitely with machines or other life-sustaining procedures.

DOCTOR CERTIFICATION: Two physicians, one of whom is the attending physician.

FOOD & WATER: No provision.

WITNESSES: Two witnesses; no notary. Form states who may not serve as a witness.

APPENDIX B:
STATE LAW
REFERENCE GUIDE

This appendix contains a state-by-state reference guide to the living wills laws. You may find all states' statutes on the Internet, although they can vary dramatically in user-friendliness. Some of these sites are maintained by the state government, while others are maintained by private companies or law firms. For some states, the laws are also available by paying for a subscription service.

The laws of all fifty states and the District of Columbia may be accessed online through **www.findlaw.com**. Once you get to the Findlaw site, go to the box headed "Search Cases & Codes" and click on "US State Resources," then click on the desired state, then click on the reference to that state's laws, such as "State Code," "Code," "Statutes," etc. Many of the sites below for individual states are the same sites that Findlaw will take you to, but they are provided here because you may wish to skip a few of the steps in getting to them through Findlaw.

These are the website addresses at the time this book was published. States sometimes change their website addresses, so if you cannot get to your state's laws with the listing below, try going through the Findlaw site. In many cases you will need to scroll down to see what you need to click on.

ALABAMA	**Website**: www.legislature.state.al.us/ALISHome.html
	[Click on desired Title, then click on desired Chapter, then click on desired Section.]
ALASKA	**Website**: www.legis.state.ak.us/folhome.htm
	[Click on desired Title.]
ARIZONA	**Website**: www.azleg.state.az.us/ArizonaRevisedStatutes.asp
ARKANSAS	**Website**: www.arkleg.state.ar.us/2003/data/ACSA.asp
	[Click on desired Title; then scroll down and click on desired Chapter; then scroll down and click on desired Section.]
CALIFORNIA	**Website**: www.leginfo.ca.gov/calaw.html
	[Click on desired Section.]
COLORADO	**Website**: http://198.187.128.12/colorado/lpext.dll?f=templates&fn=fs-main.htm&2.0
	[Click on desired Title.]
CONNECTICUT	**Website**: www.cga.state.ct.us/asp/menu/Statutes.asp
	[Click on desired Title.]
DELAWARE	**Website**: www.delcode.state.de.us
	[Click on desired Title.]
DISTRICT OF COLUMBIA	**Website**: http://dccode.westgroup.com
	[Click on "Division III Decedents' Estates and Fiduciary Relations." Click on "Title 21. Fiduciary Relations and the Mentally Ill." Click on either "Chapter 21—Uniform General Power of Attorney" or "Chapter 22—Health-Care Decisions."]

FLORIDA   **Website**: www.flsenate.gov/statutes

                       [Look for desired "Chapter" in the right-hand col-
                       umn; then click on the corresponding "Title" in the
                       left-hand column.]

GEORGIA   **Website**: www.legis.state.ga.us/cgi-bin/gl_codes_detail.pl?
                       code=1-1-1

                       [Click on desired Title; then click on desired Chapter;
                       then click on desired Section.]

HAWAII   **Website**: www.capitol.hawaii.gov/hrscurrent/?press1=docs

                       [Click on desired Chapter number.]

IDAHO   **Website**: www3.state.id.us

                       [Click on desired Title; then click on desired Chapter.
                       You may then need to click on desired Part or Section
                       number.]

ILLINOIS   **Website**: www.legis.state.il.us

                       [Click on "Illinois Compiled Statutes." Click on desired
                       Chapter number; then click on desired section number.]

INDIANA   **Website**: www.IN.gov/legislative/ic/code

                       [Click on desired Title; then click on desired Article;
                       then click on desired Chapter.]

IOWA   **Website**: www2.legis.state.ia.us

                       [Click on "Iowa Code." Type in desired Section num-
                       ber.]

KANSAS   **Website**: www.kslegislature.org

                       [Click on "Statutes." Type in desired Section number.]

KENTUCKY	**Website**: www.lrc.state.ky.us/statrev/frontpg.htm

[Click on desired Chapter number.]

LOUISIANA	**Website**: www.legis.state.la.us

[Click on "Louisiana Laws."]

[For Civil Code: In box marked "Law Body" select "CC." In box marked "Title, Article, or Rule Number" type in the desired Article number.

For Revised Statutes: In the box marked "Law Body" select "RS." In the box marked "Title, Article, or Rule Number" type in the number of the section you want that comes before the colon. In the box marked "Section Number" type in the number that comes after the colon.]

MAINE	**Website**: http://janus.state.me.us/legis/statutes

[Click on desired Title.]

MARYLAND	**Website:** www.mlis.state.md.us

[Click on + beside "Maryland Code." Click on desired code title (e.g., Health - General). Click on desired title. Click on desired section number.]

MASSACHUSETTS	**Website:** www.state.ma.us/legis/laws/mgl

[Type in desired Chapter and Section numbers.]

MICHIGAN	**Website:** http://michiganlegislature.org

[Type in desired section number.]

NOTE: *There is a separate set of books titled "Michigan Statutes Annotated," but it is outdated and should not be used.*

MINNESOTA

Website: www.leg.state.mn.us/leg/statutes.asp

[Click on desired Chapter.]

MISSISSIPPI

Website: www.sos.state.ms.us/ed_pubs/mscode

[Click on desired Title number; then click on desired Chapter number, then click on desired Section.]

MISSOURI

Website: www.moga.state.mo.us/homestat.asp

[Type in desired Statute section number.]

MONTANA

Website: www.state.mt.us/govt

[Click on "Montana Codes, Laws, and Constitution." Click on desired Title, then click on desired Chapter, then click on desired Part, then click on desired Section.]

NEBRASKA

Website: http://statutes.unicam.state.ne.us

[Select "Section Search Only" in menu, type in desired section number, and check the "Exact" search box. Then click on "View Document."]

NEVADA

Website: www.leg.state.nv.us/NRS/NRSindex

[Click on desired Chapter, then click on desired Section.]

NEW HAMPSHIRE

Website: www.state.nh.us/government/laws.html

[Click on desired Title, then click on desired Chapter, then click on desired Section.]

NEW JERSEY

Website: www.njleg.state.nj.us

[Scroll down to "Laws and Constitution" and click on "Statutes."]

New Mexico	**Website**: www.state.nm.us
	[Move cursor to "Government in NM" and click on "Laws & Statutes," then click "Statutes and Constitution of the State of New Mexico."]
New York	**Website**: http://assembly.state.ny.us/leg/?sl=0
	[Click on the desired subject (*e.g.*, "Public Health"), then click on desired Article and/or Title.]
North Carolina	**Website**: www.ncga.state.nc.us/Statutes/Statutes.asp
	[Click on desired Chapter.]
North Dakota	**Website**: www.state.nd.us/lr/information/statutes/cent-code.html
	[Scroll down to table of Titles, then click on desired Title, then click on desired Chapter.]
Ohio	**Website**: www.legislature.state.oh.us/laws.cfm
	[Click on "Ohio Revised Code." Click on desired Title, then click on desired Chapter, then click on desired Section.]
Oklahoma	**Website**: www.lsb.state.ok.us
	[Scroll down to "Legislative Information System," then click on "Oklahoma Statutes & Constitution." Locate desired Title, and click on the word "Expand;" then click on desired Section.]
Oregon	**Website**: www.leg.state.or.us/ors
	[Click on desired Chapter.]

PENNSYLVANIA   **Website**: http://members.aol.com/StatutesPA/Index.html

[Scroll down to "TABLE OF CONTENTS FOR THE PENNSYLVANIA STATUTES." Click on the desired Title, then click on the desired Chapter.]

NOTE: *No state provided online statutes database.*

RHODE ISLAND   **Website**: www.rilin.state.ri.us/statutes/statutes.html

[Click on desired Title, then click on desired Chapter, then click on desired Section.]

SOUTH CAROLINA   **Website**: www.lpitr.state.sc.us/code/statmast.htm

[Click on desired Title, then click on desired Chapter.]

SOUTH DAKOTA   **Website**: http://legis.state.sd.us

[Click on "Codified Laws." Click on desired Title, then click on desired Chapter, then click on desired Section.]

TENNESSEE   **Website**: www.tennesseeanytime.org/laws/laws.html

[Click on "Tennessee Code and Constitution," then click on + beside "Tennessee Code," then click on + beside "More...," then click on desired Title, then click on desired Chapter.]

TEXAS   **Website**: www.capitol.state.tx.us/statutes/statutes.html

[Scroll down and click on "Vernon's Texas Civil Statutes," then scroll down to click on subject (*e.g.,* Health and Safety Code), then click on desired Chapter.]

UTAH   **Website**: www.le.state.ut.us/~code/code.htm

[Click on desired Title; then click on desired Chapter, then click on desired Section.]

VERMONT   **Website**: www.leg.state.vt.us/statutes/statutes2.htm

[Click on desired Title; then click on desired Chapter; then click on desired Section.]

VIRGINIA   **Website:** http://leg1.state.va.us

[Click on "Code of Virginia," then click on "Table of Contents," then scroll down and click on desired Title, then click on desired Chapter (which has a reference to the sections); then click on desired Section.]

WASHINGTON   **Website**: www.leg.wa.gov/rcw/index.cfm

[Click on desired Title, then click on desired Chapter.]

WEST VIRGINIA   **Website**: www.legis.state.wv.us/legishp.html

[Click on "WV Code," then click on "State Code." Using the "Select Chapter" drop down menu, scroll to desired chapter number.]

WISCONSIN   **Website**: www.legis.state.wi.us/rsb/stats.html

[Click on "The Updated Wisconsin Statutes & Annotations," then scroll down and click on desired Chapter.]

WYOMING   **Website**: http://legisweb.state.wy.us/statutes/statutes.htm

[Scroll down and click on desired Title.]

APPENDIX C: FORMS

This appendix includes two types of living will forms: (1) statutory living will forms approved by various states and (2) generic forms for any state not having an approved statutory form or to supplement a state form that does not have provisions you want.

The table on page 93 will help you determine which form to use for your state. The Table of Forms on pages 94 and 95 will give you the number of the form, indicate if it is for a particular state, give the title of the form, and give the page number where that form may be found. Form numbers are found at the upper, outside edge of each form. (Remember: the law and forms may change at any time.)

If the official form for your state does not have a provision for signature before a notary, you may want to attach form 57 (**STANDARD NOTARY PAGE**) to your state form and have the signatures of yourself and your witnesses notarized. If your state's form does not have all of the provisions you would like, you may want to complete form 58 (**ADDENDUM TO LIVING WILL**) and attach it to the state form. You may attach both form 57 and form 58 to your state form if necessary.

To complete form 58, follow the instructions for form 1 on pages 24 and 25. The only difference is that, in addition to filling in your name in the first, unnumbered paragraph, you will also need to fill in the title of the living will form used in your state, and the date you signed it.

Example: If you live in Maine, the title of Maine's form is **ADVANCE HEALTH-CARE DIRECTIVE** and that title will go in the space on the second line of form 58.

Below is a state-by-state chart indicating the appropriate living will form to use.

State	Form
Alabama	3
Alaska	4
Arizona	5
Arkansas	6
California	7
Colorado	8
Connecticut	9
Delaware	10
District of Columbia	1
Florida	11 or 12
Georgia	13
Hawaii	14
Idaho	15
Illinois	16
Indiana	17 or 18*
Iowa	19
Kansas	20
Kentucky	21
Louisiana	22
Maine	23
Maryland	24
Massachusetts	1
Michigan	1
Minnesota	25
Mississippi	26
Missouri	27

State	Form
Montana	28 or 29
Nebraska	30 or 31
Nevada	32
New Hampshire	33
New Jersey	1
New Mexico	34
New York	1
North Carolina	35
North Dakota	36
Ohio	37
Oklahoma	38
Oregon	39
Pennsylvania	40
Rhode Island	41 or 42
South Carolina	43
South Dakota	44
Tennessee	45
Texas	46 or 47
Utah	48
Vermont	49
Virginia	50
Washington	51
West Virginia	52 or 53
Wisconsin	54
Wyoming	55

*Use form 15 to indicate that you **do not** want life-prolonging procedures; use form 16 to indicate that you **do want** life-prolonging procedures.

Table of Forms

LIVING WILL

I, _____, _____ (d/o/b) being of sound mind willfully and voluntarily make known my desires regarding my medical care and treatment under the circumstances as indicated below:

_____ 1. If I should have an incurable or irreversible condition that will cause my death within a relatively short time, and if I am unable to make decisions regarding my medical treatment, I direct my attending physician to withhold or withdraw procedures that merely prolong the dying process and are not necessary to my comfort or to alleviate pain. This authorization includes, but is not limited to, the withholding or the withdrawal of the following types of medical treatment (subject to any special instructions in paragraph 5 below):

    _____ a. Artificial feeding and hydration.
    _____ b. Cardiopulmonary resuscitation (this includes, but is not limited to, the use of drugs, electric shock, and artificial breathing).
    _____ c. Kidney dialysis.
    _____ d. Surgery or other invasive procedures.
    _____ e. Drugs and antibiotics.
    _____ f. Transfusions of blood or blood products.
    _____ g. Other: _____
    _____

_____ 2. If I should be in an irreversible coma or persistent vegetative state that my attending physician reasonably believes to be irreversible or incurable, I direct my attending physician to withhold or withdraw medical procedures and treatment other than such medical procedures and treatment necessary to my comfort or to alleviate pain. This authorization includes, but is not limited to, the withholding or withdrawal of the following types of medical treatment (subject to any special instructions in paragraph 5 below):

    _____ a. Artificial feeding and hydration.
    _____ b. Cardiopulmonary resuscitation (this includes, but is not limited to, the use of drugs, electric shock, and artificial breathing).
    _____ c. Kidney dialysis.
    _____ d. Surgery or other invasive procedures.
    _____ e. Drugs and antibiotics.
    _____ f. Transfusions of blood or blood products.
    _____ g. Other: _____
    _____

_____ 3. If I have a medical condition where I am unable to communicate my desires as to treatment and my physician determines that the burdens of treatment outweigh the expected benefits, I direct my attending physician to withhold or withdraw medical procedures and treatment other than such medical procedures and treatment necessary to my comfort or to alleviate pain. This authorization includes, but is not limited to, the withholding or withdrawal of the following types of medical treatment (subject to any special instructions in paragraph 5 below):

    _____ a. Artificial feeding and hydration.
    _____ b. Cardiopulmonary resuscitation (this includes, but is not limited to, the use of drugs, electric shock, and artificial breathing).
    _____ c. Kidney dialysis.
    _____ d. Surgery or other invasive procedures.
    _____ e. Drugs and antibiotics.

_____ f.　　Transfusions of blood or blood products.

_____ g.　　Other: _____

_____

_____ 4.　I want my life prolonged to the greatest extent possible (subject to any special instructions in paragraph 5 below).

_____ 5.　Special instructions (if any) _____

_____

_____

_____

Signed this _____ day of _____,200____.

_____
Signature
Address:_____

_____

The declarant is personally known to me and voluntarily signed this document in my presence.

Witness:_____　　Witness _____

Name: _____　　Name: _____

Address: _____

_____　　Address: _____

_____

State of _____　)

County of _____　)

_____

On this _____ day of _____, 200____, before me, personally appeared _____, principal, and _____and _____,

witnesses, who are personally known to me or who provided _____

as identification, and signed the foregoing instrument in my presence.

_____

Notary Public

REVOCATION OF LIVING WILL

I, _____

_____(name and address of principal), hereby revoke the

_____, which was executed by

me on _____. This revocation is effective immediately.

Date:_____

_____

Signature

State of _____   )

County of _____   )

On this _____ day of _____, 200___, before me, personally

appeared _____, who is personally known to

me or who provided _____ as identifica-

tion, and signed the foregoing instrument in my presence.

_____

Notary Public

My Commission expires:

ADVANCE DIRECTIVE FOR HEALTH CARE
(Living Will and Health Care Proxy)

This form may be used in the State of Alabama to make your wishes known about what medical treatment or other care you would or would not want if you become too sick to speak for yourself. You are not required to have an advance directive. If you do have an advance directive, be sure that your doctor, family, and friends know you have one and know where it is located.

Section 1. Living Will

I, _____, being of sound mind and at least 19 years old, would like to make the following wishes known. I direct that my family, my doctors and health care workers, and all others follow the directions I am writing down. I know that at any time I can change my mind about these directions by tearing up this form and writing a new one. I can also do away with these directions by tearing them up and by telling someone at least 19 years of age of my wishes and asking him or her to write them down.

I understand that these directions will only be used if I am not able to speak for myself.

IF I BECOME TERMINALLY ILL OR INJURED:

Terminally ill or injured is when my doctor and another doctor decide that I have a condition that cannot be cured and that I will likely die in the near future from this condition.

Life sustaining treatment - Life sustaining treatment includes drugs, machines, or medical procedures that would keep me alive but would not cure me. I know that even if I choose not to have life sustaining treatment, I will still get medicines and treatments that ease my pain and keep me comfortable.

Place your initials by either "yes" or "no":

I want to have life sustaining treatment if I am terminally ill or injured. _____ Yes _____ No

Artificially provided food and hydration (Food and water through a tube or an IV) - I understand that if I am terminally ill or injured I may need to be given food and water through a tube or an IV to keep me alive if I can no longer chew or swallow on my own or with someone helping me.

Place your initials by either "yes" or "no":

I want to have food and water provided through a tube or an IV if I am terminally ill or injured. _____ Yes _____ No

IF I BECOME PERMANENTLY UNCONSCIOUS:

Permanent unconsciousness is when my doctor and another doctor agree that within a reasonable degree of medical certainty I can no longer think, feel anything, knowingly move, or be aware of being alive. They believe this condition will last indefinitely without hope for improvement and have watched me long enough to make that decision. I understand that at least one of these doctors must be qualified to make such a diagnosis.

Life sustaining treatment - Life sustaining treatment includes drugs, machines, or other medical procedures that would keep me alive but would not cure me. I know that even if I choose not to have life sustaining treatment, I will still get medicines and treatments that ease my pain and keep me comfortable.

Place your initials by either "yes" or "no":
I want to have life-sustaining treatment if I am permanently unconscious. _____ Yes _____ No

Artificially provided food and hydration (Food and water through a tube or an IV) - I understand that if I become permanently unconscious, I may need to be given food and water through a tube or an IV to keep me alive if I can no longer chew or swallow on my own or with someone helping me.

Place your initials by either "yes" or "no":

I want to have food and water provided through a tube or an IV if I am permanently unconscious. _____ Yes _____ No

OTHER DIRECTIONS:

Please list any other things you want done or not done.

In addition to the directions I have listed on this form, I also want the following:
_____

If you do not have other directions, place your initials here: _____ No, I do not have any other directions.

Section 2. If I need someone to speak for me.

This form can be used in the State of Alabama to name a person you would like to make medical or other decisions for you if you become too sick to speak for yourself. This person is called a health care proxy. You do not have to name a health care proxy. The directions in this form will be followed even if you do not name a health care proxy.

Place your initials by only one answer:

_____ I do not want to name a health care proxy. (If you check this answer, go to Section 3)

_____ I do want the person listed below to be my health care proxy. I have talked with this person about my wishes.

First choice for proxy: _____

Relationship to me: _____

_____

City: _____ State: _____ Zip: _____

Day-time phone number: _____

Night-time phone number: _____

If this person is not able, not willing, or not available to be my health care proxy, this is my next choice:

Second choice for proxy: _____

Relationship to me: _____

Address: _____

City: _____ State: _____ Zip: _____

Day-time phone number: _____

Night-time phone number: _____

Instructions for Proxy

Place your initials by either "yes" or "no":

I want my health care proxy to make decisions about whether to give me food and water through a tube or an IV. _____ Yes _____ No

Place your initials by only one of the following:
_____ I want my health care proxy to follow only the directions as listed on this form.
_____ I want my health care proxy to follow my directions as listed on this form and to make any decisions about things I have not covered in the form.
_____ I want my health care proxy to make the final decision, even though it could mean doing something different from what I have listed on this form.

Section 3. The things listed on this form are what I want.

I understand the following:

If my doctor or hospital does not want to follow the directions I have listed, they must see that I get to a doctor or hospital who will follow my directions.

If I am pregnant, or if I become pregnant, the choices I have made on this form will not be followed until after the birth of the baby.

If the time comes for me to stop receiving life sustaining treatment or food and water through a tube or an IV, I direct that my doctor talk about the good and bad points of doing this, along with my wishes, with my health care proxy, if I have one, and with the following people:

_____

Section 4. My signature

Your name: _____

The month, day, and year of your birth: _____

Your signature: _____

Date signed: _____

Section 5. Witnesses (need two witnesses to sign)

I am witnessing this form because I believe this person to be of sound mind. I did not sign the person's signature, and I am not the health care proxy. I am not related to the person by blood, adoption, or marriage and not entitled to any part of his or her estate. I am at least 19 years of age and am not directly responsible for paying for his or her medical care.

Name of first witness: _____

Signature: _____

Date: _____

Name of second witness: _____

Signature: _____

Date: _____

Section 6. Signature of Proxy

I, _____, am willing to serve as the health care proxy.

Signature: _____ Date: _____

Signature of Second Choice for Proxy:

I, _____, am willing to serve as the health care proxy.

Signature: _____ Date: _____

DECLARATION

If I should have an incurable or irreversible condition that will cause my death within a relatively short time, it is my desire that my life not be prolonged by administration of life-sustaining procedures.

If my condition is terminal and I am unable to participate in decisions regarding my medical treatment, I direct my attending physician to withhold or withdraw procedures that merely prolong the dying process and are not necessary to my comfort or to alleviate pain.

I [   ] do [   ] do not desire that nutrition or hydration (food and water) be provided by gastric tube or intravenously if necessary.

Notwithstanding the other provisions of this declaration, if I have donated an organ under this declaration or by another method, and if I am in a hospital when a do not resuscitate order is to be implemented for me, I do not want the do not resuscitate order to take effect until the donated organ can be evaluated to determine if the organ is suitable for donation.

OPTIONAL: In the event of my death, I donate the following part(s) of my body for the purposes identified in AS 13.50.020:

Tissue:
___ Eyes   ___ Skin
___ Bone and connective tissue   ___ Heart
___ Other _____
___ Limitations _____
Organ:
___ Heart   ___ Kidney(s)   ___ Liver
___ Lung(s)   ___ Pancreas
___ Other _____

Signed this _____ day of _____, 200___.

Signature_____
Place_____

The declarant is known to me and voluntarily signed or voluntarily directed another to sign this document in my presence.

Witness_____   Witness _____

Address_____   Address _____

State of _____

_____ Judicial District

The foregoing instrument was acknowledged before me this _____ day of _____, 200___, by (name of person who acknowledged) _____.

_____   _____
Signature of Person Taking   Title or Rank
Acknowledgment
                                              _____
                                              Serial Number, if any

LIVING WILL

(Some general statements concerning your health care options are outlined below. If you agree with one of the statements, you should initial that statement. **Read all of these statements carefully before you initial your selection.** You can also write your own statement concerning life-sustaining treatment and other matters relating to your health care. You may initial any combination of paragraphs 1, 2, 3 and 4, but if you initial paragraph 5 the others should **not** be initialed.)

_____ 1. If I have a terminal condition I **do not** want my life to be prolonged and I **do not** want life-sustaining treatment, beyond comfort care, that would serve **only** to artificially delay the moment of my death.

_____ 2. If I am in a terminal condition or an irreversible coma or a persistent vegetative state that my doctors reasonably feel to be irreversible or incurable, I **do** want the medical treatment necessary to provide care that would keep me comfortable, but I **do not** want the following:

    _____ (a) Cardiopulmonary resuscitation, for example, the use of drugs, electric shock and artificial breathing.

    _____ (b) Artificially administered food and fluids.

    _____ (c) To be taken to a hospital if at all avoidable.

_____ 3. Notwithstanding my other directions, if I am known to be pregnant, I do not want life-sustaining treatment withheld or withdrawn if it is possible that the embryo/fetus will develop to the point of live birth with the continued application of life-sustaining treatment.

_____ 4. Notwithstanding my other directions I **do** want the use of all medical care necessary to treat my condition until my doctors reasonably conclude that my condition is terminal or is irreversible and incurable or I am in a persistent vegetative state.

_____ 5. I **want** my life to be prolonged to the greatest extent possible.

Other or additional statement of desires

I have _____ I have not _____ attached additional special provisions or limitations to this document to be honored in the absence of my being able to give health care directions.

_____   Date: _____
Signature of Principal   Time:_____

I hereby affirm that I was present when the principal dated and signed or marked the foregoing living will, and that the principal appeared to be of sound mind and free from duress at the time of execution of the living will; OR, that the principal was physically unable to sign or mark and that the principal directly indicated to me that the living will expressed the principal's wishes, and that the principal intended to adopt the living will at that time.

Witness:_____   Witness:_____

Address:_____   Address:_____
_____   _____

(Note: This document may be notarized instead of being witnessed.)

State of Arizona   )
County of _____   )

On this _____ day of _____, 200____, before me, personally appeared _____ (name of principal), who is personally known to me or provided _____ as identification, and acknowledged that he or she executed it.

[NOTARY SEAL]   _____
                                (signature of notary public)

DECLARATION

Initial and complete one or both of the following:

_____ If I should have an incurable or irreversible condition that will cause my death within a relatively short time, and I am no longer able to make decisions regarding my medical treatment, I direct my attending physician, pursuant to Arkansas Rights of the Terminally Ill or Permanently Unconscious Act, to [withhold or withdraw treatment that only prolongs the process of dying and is not necessary to my comfort or to alleviate pain] [follow the instructions of _____ whom I appoint as my health care proxy to decide whether life-sustaining treatment should be withheld or withdrawn].

_____ If I should become permanently unconscious I direct my attending physician, pursuant to Arkansas Rights of the Terminally Ill or Permanently Unconscious Act, to [withhold or withdraw treatment that only prolongs the process of dying and is not necessary to my comfort or to alleviate pain] [follow the instructions of _____ whom I appoint as my health care proxy to decide whether life-sustaining treatment should be withheld or withdrawn].

Initial and complete one of the following:

_____ It is my specific directive that nutrition may be withheld after consultation with my attending physician.

_____ It is my specific directive that nutrition may not be withheld.

Initial and complete one of the following:

_____ It is my specific directive that hydration may be withheld after consultation with my attending physician.

_____ It is my specific directive that hydration may not be withheld.

Signed this _____ day of _____, 200___.

Signature _____

Address _____

_____

The declarant voluntarily signed this writing in my presence.

Witness _____ Witness _____

Address _____ Address _____

ADVANCE HEALTH CARE DIRECTIVE
(California Probate Code Section 4701)

Explanation

You have the right to give instructions about your own health care. You also have the right to name someone else to make healthcare decisions for you. This form lets you do either or both of these things. It also lets you express your wishes regarding donation of organs and the designation of your primary physician. If you use this form, you may complete or modify all or any part of it.

You are free to use a different form.

Part 1 of this form is a power of attorney for health care. Part 1 lets you name another individual as agent to make health care decisions for you if you become incapable of making your own decisions or if you want someone else to make those decisions for you now even though you are still capable. You may also name an alternate agent to act for you if your first choice is not willing, able, or reasonably available to make decisions for you. (Your agent may not be an operator or employee of a community care facility or a residential care facility where you are receiving care, or your supervising health care provider or employee of the health care institution where you are receiving care, unless your agent is related to you or is a coworker.)

Unless the form you sign limits the authority of your agent, your agent may make all health care decisions for you. This form has a place for you to limit the authority of your agent. You need not limit the authority of your agent if you wish to rely on your agent for all health care decisions that may have to be made. If you choose not to limit the authority of your agent, your agent will have the right to:
   (a) Consent or refuse consent to any care, treatment, service, or procedure to maintain, diagnose, or otherwise affect a physical or mental condition.
   (b) Select or discharge health care providers and institutions.
   (c) Approve or disapprove diagnostic tests, surgical procedures, and programs of medication.
   (d) Direct the provision, withholding, or withdrawal of artificial nutrition and hydration and all other forms of health care, including cardiopulmonary resuscitation.
   (e) Make anatomical gifts, authorize an autopsy, and direct disposition of remains.

Part 2 of this form lets you give specific instructions about any aspect of your health care, whether or not you appoint an agent. Choices are provided for you to express your wishes regarding the provision, withholding, or withdrawal of treatment to keep you alive, as well as the provision of pain relief. Space is also provided for you to add to the choices you have made or for you to write out any additional wishes. If you are satisfied to allow your agent to determine what is best for you in making end-of-life decisions, you need not fill out Part 2 of this form.

Part 3 of this form lets you express an intention to donate your bodily organs and tissues following your death.

Part 4 of this form lets you designate a physician to have primary responsibility for your health care.

After completing this form, sign and date the form at the end. The form must be signed by two qualified witnesses or acknowledged before a notary public. Give a copy of the signed and completed form to your physician, to any other health care providers you may have, to any health care institution at which you are receiving care, and to any health care agents you have named. You should talk to the person you have named as agent to make sure that he or she understands your wishes and is willing to take the responsibility.

You have the right to revoke this advance health care directive or replace this form at any time.

PART 1
POWER OF ATTORNEY FOR HEALTH CARE

(1.1) DESIGNATION OF AGENT: I designate the following individual as my agent to make health care decisions for me:

_____
(name of individual you choose as agent)

_____
(address)   (city)   (state)   (zip code)

_____
(home phone)   (work phone)

OPTIONAL: If I revoke my agent's authority or if my agent is not willing, able, or reasonably available to make a health care decision for me, I designate as my first alternate agent:

_____
(name of individual you choose as first alternate agent)

_____
(address)   (city)   (state)   (zip code)

_____
(home phone)   (work phone)

OPTIONAL: If I revoke the authority of my agent and first alternate agent or if neither is willing, able, or reasonably available to make a health care decision for me, I designate as my second alternate agent:

_____
(name of individual you choose as second alternate agent)

_____
(address)   (city)   (state)   (zip code)

_____
(home phone)   (work phone)

(1.2) AGENT'S AUTHORITY: My agent is authorized to make all health care decisions for me, including decisions to provide, withhold, or withdraw artificial nutrition and hydration and all other forms of health care to keep me alive, except as I state here:

_____
_____
_____
(Add additional sheets if needed.)

(1.3) WHEN AGENT'S AUTHORITY BECOMES EFFECTIVE: My agent's authority becomes effective when my primary physician determines that I am unable to make my own health care decisions unless I mark the following box.

If I mark this box (   ), my agent's authority to make health care decisions for me takes effect immediately.

(1.4) AGENT'S OBLIGATION: My agent shall make health care decisions for me in accordance with this power of attorney for health care, any instructions I give in Part 2 of this form, and my other wishes to the extent known to my agent. To the extent my wishes are unknown, my agent shall make health care decisions for me in accordance with what my agent determines to be in my best interest. In determining my best interest, my agent shall consider my personal values to the extent known to my agent.

(1.5) AGENT'S POSTDEATH AUTHORITY: My agent is authorized to make anatomical gifts, authorize an autopsy, and direct disposition of my remains, except as I state here or in Part 3 of this form:_____

_____
_____
(Add additional sheets if needed.)

(1.6) NOMINATION OF CONSERVATOR: If a conservator of my person needs to be appointed for me by a court, I nominate the agent designated in this form. If that agent is not willing, able, or reasonably available to act as conservator, I nominate the alternate agents whom I have named, in the order designated.

PART 2
INSTRUCTIONS FOR HEALTH CARE

If you fill out this part of the form, you may strike any wording you do not want.

(2.1) END-OF-LIFE DECISIONS: I direct that my health care providers and others involved in my care provide, withhold, or withdraw treatment in accordance with the choice I have marked below:

☐ (a) Choice Not To Prolong Life

I do not want my life to be prolonged if (1) I have an incurable and irreversible condition that will result in my death within a relatively short time, (2) I become unconscious and, to a reasonable degree of medical certainty, I will not regain consciousness, or (3) the likely risks and burdens of treatment would outweigh the expected benefits, OR

☐ (b) Choice To Prolong Life

I want my life to be prolonged as long as possible within the limits of generally accepted health care standards.

(2.2) RELIEF FROM PAIN: Except as I state in the following space, I direct that treatment for alleviation of pain or discomfort be provided at all times, even if it hastens my death:

_____

_____

(Add additional sheets if needed.)

(2.3) OTHER WISHES: (If you do not agree with any of the optional choices above and wish to write your own, or if you wish to add to the instructions you have given above, you may do so here.) I direct that:

_____

_____

(Add additional sheets if needed.)

PART 3
DONATION OF ORGANS AT DEATH
(OPTIONAL)

(3.1) Upon my death (mark applicable box):

☐ (a) I give any needed organs, tissues, or parts, OR

☐ (b) I give the following organs, tissues, or parts only:

_____

(c) My gift is for the following purposes (strike any of the following you do not want):

(1) Transplant
(2) Therapy
(3) Research
(4) Education

PART 4
PRIMARY PHYSICIAN
(OPTIONAL)

(4.1) I designate the following physician as my primary physician:

_____
(name of physician)

_____
(address)   (city)   (state)   (zip code)

_____
(phone)

OPTIONAL: If the physician I have designated above is not willing, able, or reasonably available to act as my primary physician, I designate the following physician as my primary physician:

_____
(name of physician)

_____
(address)   (city)   (state)   (zip code)

_____
(phone)

PART 5

(5.1) EFFECT OF COPY: A copy of this form has the same effect as the original.

(5.2) SIGNATURE: Sign and date the form here:

_____   _____
(date)   (sign your name)

_____   _____
(address)   (print your name)

_____
(city)   (state)

(5.3) STATEMENT OF WITNESSES: I declare under penalty of perjury under the laws of California (1) that the individual who signed or acknowledged this advance health care directive is personally known to me, or that the individual's identity was proven to me by convincing evidence (2) that the individual signed or acknowledged this advance directive in my presence, (3) that the individual appears to be of sound mind and under no duress, fraud, or undue influence, (4) that I am not a person appointed as agent by this advance directive, and (5) that I am not the individual's health care provider, an employee of the individual's health care provider, the operator of a community care facility, an employee of an operator of a of a community care facility, the operator of a residential care facility for the elderly, nor an employee of an operator of a residential care facility for the elderly.

First witness   Second witness

_____   _____
(print name)   (print name)

_____   _____
(address)   (address)

_____   _____
(city)   (state)   (city)   (state)

_____   _____
(signature of witness)   (signature of witness)

_____   _____
(date)   (date)

(5.4) ADDITIONAL STATEMENT OF WITNESSES: At least one of the above witnesses must also sign the following declaration:

I further declare under penalty of perjury under the laws of California that I am not related to the individual executing this advance health care directive by blood, marriage, or adoption, and to the best of my knowledge, I am not entitled to any part of the individual's estate upon his or her death under a will now existing or by operation of law.

_____   _____
(signature of witness)   (signature of witness)

PART 6
SPECIAL WITNESS REQUIREMENT

(6.1) The following statement is required only if you are a patient in a skilled nursing facility--a health care facility that provides the following basic services: skilled nursing care and supportive care to patients whose primary need is for availability of skilled nursing care on an extended basis. The patient advocate or ombudsman must sign the following statement:

STATEMENT OF PATIENT ADVOCATE OR OMBUDSMAN

I declare under penalty of perjury under the laws of California that I am a patient advocate or ombudsman as designated by the State Department of Aging and that I am serving as a witness as required by Section 4675 of the Probate Code.

_____   _____
(date)   (sign your name)

_____   _____
(address)   (print your name)

_____
(city)   (state)

DECLARATION AS TO MEDICAL OR SURGICAL TREATMENT

I, _____, being of sound mind and at least eighteen years of age, direct that my life shall not be artificially prolonged under the circumstances set forth below and hereby declare that:

1. If at any time my attending physician and one other qualified physician certify in writing that:

    a. I have an injury, disease, or illness which is not curable or reversible and which, in their judgment, is a terminal condition, and

    b. For a period of seven consecutive days or more, I have been unconscious, comatose, or otherwise incompetent so as to be unable to make or communicate responsible decisions concerning my person, then

I direct that, in accordance with Colorado law, life-sustaining procedures shall be withdrawn and withheld pursuant to the terms of this declaration, it being understood that life-sustaining procedures shall not include any medical procedure or intervention for nourishment considered necessary by the attending physician to provide comfort or alleviate pain. However, I may specifically direct, in accordance with Colorado law, that artificial nourishment be withdrawn or withheld pursuant to the terms of this declaration.

2. In the event that the only procedure I am being provided is artificial nourishment, I direct that one of the following actions be taken:

_____ a. Artificial nourishment shall not be continued when it is the only procedure being provided; or

_____ b. Artificial nourishment shall be continued for _____ days when it is the only procedure being provided; or

_____ c. Artificial nourishment shall be continued when it is the only procedure being provided.

3. I execute this declaration, as my free and voluntary act, this _____ day of _____, 200___.

By_____
Declarant

The foregoing instrument was signed and declared by _____ to be his declaration, in the presence of us, who, in his presence, in the presence of each other, and at his request, have signed our names below as witnesses, and we declare that, at the time of the execution of this instrument, the declarant, according to our best knowledge and belief, was of sound mind and under no constraint or undue influence.

Dated at _____, Colorado, this _____ day of _____, 200___.

_____
Name and Address of Witness

_____
Name and Address of Witness

STATE OF COLORADO   )
) ss.
COUNTY OF _____   )

SUBSCRIBED and sworn to before me by _____, the declarant, and _____ and _____, witnesses, as the voluntary act and deed of the declarant the _____ day of _____, 200____.
My commission expires:

_____
Notary Public

DOCUMENT CONCERNING WITHHOLDING OR WITHDRAWAL OF LIFE SUPPORT SYSTEMS

If the time comes when I am incapacitated to the point when I can no longer actively take part in decisions for my own life, and am unable to direct my physicians as to my own medical care, I wish this statement to stand as a testament of my wishes.

I, _____ (Name), request that, if my condition is deemed terminal or if it is determined that I will be permanently unconscious, I be allowed to die and not be kept alive through life support systems. By terminal condition, I mean that I have an incurable or irreversible medical condition which, without the administration of life support systems, will, in the opinion of my attending physician, result in death within a relatively short time. By permanently unconscious I mean that I am in a permanent coma or persistent vegetative state which is an irreversible condition in which I am at no time aware of myself or the environment and show no behavioral response to the environment. The life support systems which I do not want include, but are not limited to:

- Artificial respiration   • Cardiopulmonary resuscitation

- Artificial means of providing nutrition and hydration

(Cross out and initial life support systems you want administered)

I do not intend any direct taking of my life, but only that my dying not be unreasonably prolonged.

Other specific requests:

_____

_____.

This request is made, after careful reflection, while I am of sound mind.

_____

Signature

_____ Date

This document was signed in our presence, by the above-named _____ _____ (Name) who appeared to be eighteen years of age or older, of sound mind and able to understand the nature and consequences of health care decisions at the time the document was signed.

_____ Witness   _____ Witness

_____ Address   _____ Address

ADVANCE HEALTH CARE DIRECTIVE

Explanation

You have the right to give instructions about your own health care. You also have the right to name someone else to make health-care decisions for you. This form lets you do either or both of these things. It also lets you express your wishes regarding anatomical gifts and the designation of your primary physician. If you use this form, you may complete or modify all or any part of it. You are free to use a different form.

Part 1 of this form is a power of attorney for health care. Part 1 lets you name another individual as agent to make health-care decisions for you if you become incapable of making your own decisions. You may also name an alternate agent to act for you if your first choice is not willing, able or reasonably available to make decisions for you. Unless related to you, an agent may not have a controlling interest in or be an operator or employee of a residential long-term health-care institution at which you are receiving care. If you do not have a qualifying condition (terminal illness/injury or permanent unconsciousness), your agent may make all health-care decisions for you except for decisions providing, withholding or withdrawing of a life sustaining procedure.

Unless you limit the agent's authority, your agent will have the right to:

(a) Consent or refuse consent to any care, treatment, service or procedure to maintain, diagnose or otherwise affect a physical or mental condition unless it's a life-sustaining procedure or otherwise required by law.

(b) Select or discharge health-care providers and health-care institutions;

If you have a qualifying condition, your agent may make all health-care decisions for you, including, but not limited to:

(c) The decisions listed in (a) and (b).

(d) Consent or refuse consent to life sustaining procedures, such as, but not limited to, cardiopulmonary resuscitation and orders not to resuscitate.

(e) Direct the providing, withholding or withdrawal of artificial nutrition and hydration and all other forms of health care.

Part 2 of this form lets you give specific instructions about any aspect of your health care. Choices are provided for you to express your wishes regarding the provision, withholding or withdrawal of treatment to keep you alive, including the provision of artificial nutrition and hydration as well as the provision of pain relief. Space is also provided for you to add to the choices you have made or for you to write out any additional instructions for other than end of life decisions.

Part 3 of this form lets you express an intention to donate your bodily organs and tissues following your death.

Part 4 of this form lets you designate a physician to have primary responsibility for your health care.

After completing this form, sign and date the form at the end. It is required that 2 other individuals sign as witnesses. Give a copy of the signed and completed form to your physician, to any other health-care providers you may have, to any health-care institution at which you are receiving care and to any health-care agents you have named. You should talk to the person you have named as agent to make sure that the person understands your wishes and is willing to take the responsibility.

You have the right to revoke this advance health-care directive or replace this form at any time.

* *

PART 1: POWER OF ATTORNEY FOR HEALTH CARE

(1) DESIGNATION OF AGENT: I designate the following individual as my agent to make health-care decisions for me:

_____

(name of individual you choose as agent)

_____

(address)   (city)   (state)   (zip code)

_____

(home phone)   (work phone)

OPTIONAL: If I revoke my agent's authority or if my agent is not willing, able or reasonably available to make a health-care decision for me, I designate as my first alternate agent:

_____

(name of individual you choose as first alternate agent)

_____

(address)   (city)   (state)   (zip code)

_____

(home phone)   (work phone)

OPTIONAL: If I revoke the authority of my agent and first alternate agent or if neither is willing, able or reasonably available to make a health-care decision for me, I designate as my second alternate agent:

_____

(name of individual you choose as second alternate agent)

_____

(address)   (city)   (state)   (zip code)

_____

(home phone)   (work phone)

(2) AGENT'S AUTHORITY: If I am not in a qualifying condition my agent is authorized to make all health-care decisions for me, except decisions about life-sustaining procedures and as I state here; and if I am in a qualifying condition, my agent is authorized to make all health-care decisions for me, except as I state here:

_____

_____

(Add additional sheets if needed.)

(3) WHEN AGENT'S AUTHORITY BECOMES EFFECTIVE: My agent's authority becomes effective when my primary physician determines I lack the capacity to make my own health-care decisions. As to decisions concerning the providing, withholding and withdrawal of life-sustaining procedures my agent's authority becomes effective when my primary physician determines I lack the capacity to make my own health-care decisions and my primary physician and another physician determine that I am in a terminal condition or permanently unconscious.

(4) AGENT'S OBLIGATIONS: My agent shall make health-care decisions for me in accordance with this power of attorney for health care, any instructions I give in Part 2 of this form, and my other wishes to the extent known to my agent. To the extent my wishes are unknown, my agent shall make health-care decisions for me in accordance with what my agent determines to be in my best interest. In determining my best interest, my agent shall consider my personal values to the extent known to my agent.

(5) NOMINATION OF GUARDIAN: If a guardian of my person needs to be appointed for me by a court, (please check one):

[   ] I nominate the agent(s) whom I named in this form in the order designated to act as guardian.

[   ] I nominate the following to be guardian in the order designated: _____

_____

[   ] I do not nominate anyone to be guardian.

PART 2. INSTRUCTIONS FOR HEALTH CARE

If you are satisfied to allow your agent to determine what is best for you in making end-of-life decisions, you need not fill out this part of the form. If you do fill out this part of the form, you may strike any wording you do not want.

(6) END-OF-LIFE DECISIONS: If I am in a qualifying condition, I direct that my health-care providers and others involved in my care provide, withhold, or withdraw treatment in accordance with the choice I have marked below:

Choice Not To Prolong Life

I do not want my life to be prolonged if: (please check all that apply)

_____ (i) I have a terminal condition (an incurable condition caused by injury, disease, or illness which, to a reasonable degree of medical certainty, makes death imminent and from which, despite the application of life-sustaining procedures, there can be no recovery) and regarding artificial nutrition and hydration,

I make the following specific directions:	I want used	I do not want used
Artificial nutrition through a conduit	_____	_____
Hydration through a conduit	_____	_____

_____ (ii) I become permanently unconscious (a medical condition that has been diagnosed in accordance with currently accepted medical standards that has lasted at least 4 weeks and with reasonable medical certainty as total and irreversible loss of consciousness and capacity for interaction with the environment. The term includes, without limitation, a persistent vegetative state or irreversible coma) and regarding artificial nutrition and hydration,

I make the following specific directions:	I want used	I do not want used
Artificial nutrition through a conduit	_____	_____
Hydration through a conduit	_____	_____

Choice To Prolong Life

_____ I want my life to be prolonged as long as possible within the limits of generally accepted health-care standards.

RELIEF FROM PAIN: Except as I state in the following space, I direct treatment for alleviation of pain or discomfort be provided at all times, even if it hastens my death: _____

_____

_____

(7) OTHER MEDICAL INSTRUCTIONS: (If you do not agree with any of the optional choices above and wish to write you own, or if you wish to add to the instructions you have given above, you may do so here.) I direct that:

_____

_____

(Add additional sheets if necessary.)

PART 3: ANATOMICAL GIFTS AT DEATH
(OPTIONAL)

(8) I am mentally competent and 18 years or more of age.

I hereby make this anatomical gift to take effect upon my death. The marks in the appropriate squares and words filled into the blanks below indicate my desires.

I give: [   ] my body;   [   ] any needed organs or parts;

[   ] the following organs or parts: _____

To the following person or institutions:

[   ] the physician in attendance at my death;

[   ] the hospital in which I die;

[   ] the following named physician, hospital, storage bank or other medical institution:

_____

[   ] the following individual for treatment:

_____

for the following purposes: [   ] any purpose authorized by law; [   ] transplantation;

[   ] therapy;   [   ] research;   [   ] medical education.

PART 4: PRIMARY PHYSICIAN
(OPTIONAL)

(9) I designate the following physician as my primary physician:

_____

(name of physician)   (phone)

_____

(address)   (city)   (state)   (zip code)

OPTIONAL: If the physician I have designated above is not willing, able or reasonably available to act as my primary physician, I designate the following physician as my primary physician:

_____

(name of physician)   (phone)

_____

(address)   (city)   (state)   (zip code)

Primary Physician shall mean a physician designated by an individual or the individual's agent or guardian, to have primary responsibility for the individual's health care or, in the absence of a designation or if the designated physician is not reasonably available, a physician who undertakes the responsibility.

* * * * * * * * * * * * * * * * * * * *

(10) EFFECT OF COPY: A copy of this form has the same effect as the original.

(11) SIGNATURE: Sign and date the form here: I understand the purposes and effect of this document.

_____   _____

(date)   (sign your name)

_____   _____

(address)   (print your name)

_____   _____

(city)   (state)   (zip code)

(12) SIGNATURE OF WITNESSES:

Statement Of Witnesses

SIGNED AND DECLARED by the above-named declarant as and for his/her written declaration under 16 Del.C. §§ 2502 and 2503, in our presence, who in his/her presence, at his/her request, and in the presence of each other, have hereunto subscribed our names as witnesses, and state:

A. That the Declarant is mentally competent.
B. That neither of them:
  1. Is related to the declarant by blood, marriage or adoption;
  2. Is entitled to any portion of the estate of the declarant under any will of the declarant or codicil thereto then existing nor, at the time of the executing of the advance health care directive, is so entitled by operation of law then existing;
  3. Has, at the time of the execution of the advance health-care directive, a present or inchoate claim against any portion of the estate of the declarant;
  4. Has a direct financial responsibility for the declarant's medical care;
  5. Has a controlling interest in or is an operator or an employee of a residential long-term health-care institution in which the declarant is a resident; or
  6. Is under eighteen years of age.
C. That if the declarant is a resident of a sanitarium, rest home, nursing home, boarding home or related institution, one of the witnesses, _____, is at the time of the execution of the advance health-care directive, a patient advocate or ombudsman designated by the Division of Services for Aging and Adults with Physical Disabilities or the Public Guardian.

First witness

_____
(print name)

_____
(address)

_____
(city)   (state)

_____
(signature of witness)

_____
(date)

I am not prohibited by § 2503 of Title 16 of the Delaware Code from being a witness.

Second witness

_____
(print name)

_____
(address)

_____
(city)   (state)

_____
(signature of witness)

_____
(date)

I am not prohibited by § 2503 of Title 16 of the Delaware Code from being a witness.

LIVING WILL

Declaration made this _____ day of _____, 200_____
I, _____, willfully and voluntarily make known
my desire that my dying not be artificially prolonged under the circumstances set forth below, and I
do hereby declare, that if at any time I am incapacitated and

_____ (initial) I have a terminal condition or

_____ (initial) I have an end-state condition or

_____ (initial) I am in a persistent vegetative state

and if my attending or treating physician and another consulting physician have determined that
there is no reasonable medical probability of my recovery from such condition, I direst that life-prolonging procedures be withheld or withdrawn when the application of such procedures would serve
only to prolong artificially the process of dying, and that I be permitted to die naturally with only the
administration of medication or the performance of any medical procedure deemed necessary to provide me with comfort care or to alleviate pain.

It is my intention that this declaration be honored by my family and physician as the final expression of my legal right to refuse medical or surgical treatment and to accept the consequences for such
refusal.

In the event that I have been determined to be unable to provide express and informed consent
regarding the withholding, withdrawal, or continuation of life-prolonging procedures, I wish to designate, as my surrogate to carry out the provisions of this declaration:

Name: _____

Address:_____

Zip Code:_____   Phone:_____

I understand the full import of this declaration, and I am emotionally and mentally competent to
make this declaration.

Additional Instructions (optional):_____

_____

_____

Signed

Witness: _____   Witness: _____

Name: _____   Name: _____

Address: _____   Address: _____

_____   _____

Phone: _____   Phone: _____

DESIGNATION OF HEALTH CARE SURROGATE

Name:_____(Last)_____(First)_____(Middle Initial)

In the event that I have been determined to be incapacitated to provide informed consent for medical treatment and surgical and diagnostic procedures, I wish to designate as my surrogate for health care decisions:

Name: _____

Address: _____

_____Zip Code:_____

Phone:_____

If my surrogate is unwilling or unable to perform his or her duties, I wish to designate as my alternate surrogate:

Name: _____

Address: _____

_____Zip Code:_____

Phone:_____

I fully understand that this designation will permit my designee to make health care decisions, except for anatomical gifts, unless I have executed an anatomical gift declaration pursuant to law, and to provide, withhold, or withdraw consent on my behalf; to apply for public benefits to defray the cost of health care; and to authorize my admission to or transfer from a health care facility.

Additional instructions (optional):

_____

_____

_____

I further affirm that this designation is not being made as a condition of treatment or admission to a health care facility. I will notify and send a copy of this document to the following persons other than my surrogate, so they may know who my surrogate is.

Name: _____

Name: _____

Signed: _____

Date: _____

Witnesses:

1._____

2._____

LIVING WILL

Living will made this _____ day of _____, 200___.

I, _____, being of sound mind, willfully and voluntarily make known my desire that my life shall not be prolonged under the circumstances set forth below and do declare:

1. If at any time I should (check each option desired):

    (   )   have a terminal condition,

    (   )   become in a coma with no reasonable expectation of regaining consciousness, or

    (   )   become in a permanent vegetative state with no reasonable expectation of regaining significant cognitive function,

as defined in and established in accordance with the procedures set forth in paragraphs (2), (9), and (13) of Code Section 31-32-2 of the Official Code of Georgia Annotated, I direct that the application of life-sustaining procedures to my body (check the option desired):

    (   )   including nourishment and hydration,

    (   )   including nourishment but not hydration, or

    (   )   excluding nourishment and hydration,

be withheld or withdrawn and that I be permitted to die;

2. In the absence of my ability to give directions regarding the use for such life-sustaining procedures, it is my intention that this living will shall be honored by my family and physician(s) as the final expression of my legal right to refuse medical or surgical treatment and accept the consequences from such refusal;

3. I understand that I may revoke this living will at any time;

4. I understand the full import of this living will, and I am at least 18 years of age and am emotionally and mentally competent to make this living will; and

5. If I am a female and I have been diagnosed as pregnant, this living will shall have no force and effect unless the fetus is not viable and I indicate by initialing after this sentence that I want this living will to be carried out.   _____ (Initial)

Signed _____

_____ (City), _____ (County),

and _____ (State of Residence).

I hereby witness this living will and attest that:

(1)　The declarant is personally known to me and I believe the declarant to be at least 18 years of age and of sound mind;

(2)　I am at least 18 years of age;

(3)　To the best of my knowledge, at the time of the execution of this living will, I:

    (A)　Am not related to the declarant by blood or marriage;

    (B)　Would not be entitled to any portion of the declarant's estate by any will or by operation of law under the rules of descent and distribution of this state;

    (C)　Am not the attending physician of declarant or an employee of the attending physician or an employee of the hospital or skilled nursing facility in which declarant is a patient;

    (D)　Am not directly financially responsible for the declarant's medical care; and

    (E)　Have no present claim against any portion of the estate of the declarant;

(4)　Declarant has signed this document in my presence as above instructed, on the date above first shown.

Witness _____   Witness _____

Address _____   Address _____

_____   _____

Additional witness required when living will is signed in a hospital or skilled nursing facility.

I hereby witness this living will and attest that I believe the declarant to be of sound mind and to have made this living will willingly and voluntarily.

Witness: _____

Medical director of skilled nursing facility or staff physician not participating in care of the patient or chief of the hospital medical staff or staff physician or hospital designee not participating in care of the patient.

ADVANCE HEALTH CARE DIRECTIVE

Explanation

You have the right to give instructions about your own health care. You also have the right to name someone else to make health-care decisions for you. This form lets you do either or both of these things. It also lets you express your wishes regarding the designation of your health-care provider. If you use this form, you may complete or modify all or any part of it. You are free to use a different form.

Part 1 of this form is a power of attorney for health care. Part 1 lets you name another individual as agent to make health-care decisions for you if you become incapable of making your own decisions or if you want someone else to make those decisions for you now even though you are still capable. You may name an alternate agent to act for you if your first choice is not willing, able, or reasonably available to make decisions for you. Unless related to you, your agent may not be an owner, operator, or employee of a health-care institution where you are receiving care.

Unless the form you sign limits the authority of your agent, your agent may make all health-care decisions for you. This form has a place for you to limit the authority of your agent. You need not limit the authority of your agent if you wish to rely on your agent for all health-care decisions that may have to be made. If you choose not to limit the authority of your agent, your agent will have the right to:

(1) Consent or refuse consent to any care, treatment, service, or procedure to maintain, diagnose, or otherwise affect a physical or mental condition;

(2) Select or discharge health-care providers and institutions;

(3) Approve or disapprove diagnostic tests, surgical procedures, programs of medication, and orders not to resuscitate; and

(4) Direct the provision, withholding, or withdrawal of artificial nutrition and hydration and all other forms of health care.

Part 2 of this form lets you give specific instructions about any aspect of your health care. Choices are provided for you to express your wishes regarding the provision, withholding, or withdrawal of treatment to keep you alive, including the provision of artificial nutrition and hydration, as well as the provision of pain relief medication. Space is also provided for you to add to the choices you have made or for you to write out any additional wishes.

Part 3 of this form lets you express an intention to donate your bodily organs and tissues following your death.

Part 4 of this form lets you designate a physician to have primary responsibility for your health care.

After completing this form, sign and date the form at the end and have the form witnessed by one of the two alternative methods listed below. Give a copy of the signed and completed form to your physician, to any other health-care providers you may have, to any health-care institution at which you are receiving care, and to any health-care agents you have named. You should talk to the person you have named as agent to make sure that he or she understands your wishes and is willing to take the responsibility.

You have the right to revoke this advance health-care directive or replace this form at any time.

* * * * * * * * * * * * * * * * * * *

PART 1. DURABLE POWER OF ATTORNEY FOR HEALTH-CARE DECISIONS

(1) DESIGNATION OF AGENT: I designate the following individual as my agent to make health-care decisions for me:

_____

(name of individual you choose as agent)

_____

(address)   (city)   (state)   (zip code)

_____

(home phone)   (work phone)

OPTIONAL: If I revoke my agent's authority or if my agent is not willing, able, or reasonably available to make a health-care decision for me, I designate as my first alternate agent:

_____

(name of individual you choose as first alternate agent)

_____

(address)   (city)   (state)   (zip code)

_____

(home phone)   (work phone)

OPTIONAL: If I revoke the authority of my agent and first alternate agent or if neither is willing, able, or reasonably available to make a health-care decision for me, I designate as my second alternate agent:

_____

(name of individual you choose as second alternate agent)

_____

(address)   (city)   (state)   (zip code)

_____

(home phone)   (work phone)

(2) AGENT'S AUTHORITY: My agent is authorized to make all health-care decisions for me, including decisions to provide, withhold, or withdraw artificial nutrition and hydration, and all other forms of health care to keep me alive, except as I state here:

_____

_____

_____

(Add additional sheets if needed)

(3) WHEN AGENT'S AUTHORITY BECOMES EFFECTIVE: My agent's authority becomes effective when my primary physician determines that I am unable to make my own health-care decisions unless I mark the following box. If I mark this box [ ], my agent's authority to make health-care decisions for me takes effect immediately.

(4) AGENT'S OBLIGATION: My agent shall make health-care decisions for me in accordance with this power of attorney for health care, any instructions I give in Part 2 of this form, and my other wishes to the extent known to my agent. To the extent my wishes are unknown, my agent shall make health-care decisions for me in accordance with what my agent determines to be in my best interest. In determining my best interest, my agent shall consider my personal values to the extent known to my agent.

(5) NOMINATION OF GUARDIAN: If a guardian of my person needs to be appointed for me by a court, I nominate the agent designated in this form. If that agent is not willing, able, or reasonably available to act as guardian, I nominate the alternate agents whom I have named, in the order designated.

PART 2. INSTRUCTIONS FOR HEALTH CARE

If you are satisfied to allow your agent to determine what is best for you in making end-of-life decisions, you need not fill out this part of the form. If you do fill out this part of the form, you may strike any wording you do not want.

(6) END-OF-LIFE DECISIONS: I direct that my health-care providers and others involved in my care provide, withhold, or withdraw treatment in accordance with the choice I have marked below:
(Check only one box):

[ ] (a) Choice Not To Prolong Life: I do not want my life to be prolonged if (i) I have an incurable and irreversible condition that will result in my death within a relatively short time, (ii) I become unconscious and, to a reasonable degree of medical certainty, I will not regain consciousness, or (iii) the likely risks and burdens of treatment would outweigh the expected benefits, OR

[ ] (b) Choice To Prolong Life: I want my life to be prolonged as long as possible within the limits of generally accepted health-care standards.

(7) ARTIFICIAL NUTRITION AND HYDRATION: Artificial nutrition and hydration must be provided, withheld or withdrawn in accordance with the choice I have made in paragraph (6) unless I mark the following box. If I mark this box [ ], artificial nutrition and hydration must be provided regardless of my condition and regardless of the choice I have made in paragraph (6).

(8) RELIEF FROM PAIN: If I mark this box [ ], I direct that treatment to alleviate pain or discomfort be provided to me even if it hastens my death.

(9) OTHER WISHES: (If you do not agree with any of the optional choices above and wish to write your own, or if you wish to add to the instructions you have given above, you may do so here.) I direct that:

_____

_____

(Add additional sheets if needed)

PART 3. DONATION OF ORGANS AT DEATH (OPTIONAL)

(10) Upon my death (mark applicable box)

[ ] (a) I give any needed organs, tissues, or parts OR
[ ] (b) I give the following organs, tissues, or parts only

_____

[ ] (c) My gift is for the following purposes (strike any of the following you do not want)
(i) Transplant
(ii) Therapy
(iii) Research
(iv) Education

PART 4. PRIMARY PHYSICIAN (OPTIONAL)

(11) I designate the following physician as my primary physician:

_____
(name of physician) (phone)

_____
(address) (city) (state) (zip code)

OPTIONAL: If the physician I have designated above is not willing, able, or reasonably available to act as my primary physician, I designate the following physician as my primary physician:

_____
(name of physician) (phone)

_____
(address) (city) (state) (zip code)

* * * * * * * * * * * * * * * * * * * *

(12)   EFFECT OF COPY: A copy of this form has the same effect as the original.

(13)   SIGNATURES: Sign and date the form here:

_____   _____
                (date)   (sign your name)

_____   _____
              (address)   (print your name)

_____
      (city)   (state)

(14)   WITNESSES: This power of attorney will not be valid for making health-care decisions unless it is either (a) signed by two qualified adult witnesses who are personally known to you and who are present when you sign or acknowledge your signature; or (b) acknowledged before a notary public in the State.

ALTERNATIVE NO. 1

Witness

I declare under penalty of false swearing pursuant to section 710-1062, Hawaii Revised Statutes, that the principal is personally known to me, that the principal signed or acknowledged this power of attorney in my presence, that the principal appears to be of sound mind and under no duress, fraud, or undue influence, that I am not the person appointed as agent in this document, and that I am not a health-care provider, nor an employee of a health-care provider or facility. I am not related to the principal by blood, marriage, or adoption, and to the best of my knowledge, I am not entitled to any part of the estate of the principal upon the death of the principal under a will now existing or by operation of law.

_____   _____
                (date)   (sign your name)

_____   _____
              (address)   (print your name)

_____
      (city)   (state)

Witness

I declare under penalty of false swearing pursuant to section 710-1062, Hawaii Revised Statutes, that the principal is personally known to me, that the principal signed or acknowledged this power of attorney in my presence, that the principal appears to be of sound mind and under no duress, fraud, or undue influence, that I am not the person appointed as agent in this document, and that I am not a health-care provider, nor an employee of a health-care provider or facility.

_____   _____
                (date)   (sign your name)

_____   _____
              (address)   (print your name)

_____
      (city)   (state)

ALTERNATIVE NO. 2

State of Hawaii

County of _____

On this _____ day of _____, in the year _____, before me, _____ _____ (insert name of notary public) appeared _____ _____, personally known to me (or proved to me on the basis of satisfactory evidence) to be the person whose name is subscribed to this instrument, and acknowledged that he or she executed it.

Notary Seal

_____
(Signature of Notary Public)

A LIVING WILL

A Directive to Withhold or to Provide Treatment

To my family, my relatives, my friends, my physicians, my employers, and all others whom it may concern:

Directive made this _____ day of _____, 200____, I, _____

_____(name), being of sound mind, willfully, and voluntarily make known my desire that my life shall not be prolonged artificially under the circumstances set forth below, do hereby declare:

    1.   If at any time I should have an incurable injury, disease, illness or condition certified to be terminal by two medical doctors who have examined me, and where the application of life-sustaining procedures of any kind would serve only to prolong artificially the moment of my death, and where a medical doctor determines that my death is imminent, whether or not life-sustaining procedures are utilized, or I have been diagnosed as being in a persistent vegetative state, I direct that the following marked expressions of my intent be followed and that I be permitted to die naturally, and that I receive any medical treatment or care that may be required to keep me free of pain or distress.

    Check One Box.

    ☐   If at any time I should become unable to communicate my instructions, then I direct that all medical treatment, care, and nutrition and hydration necessary to restore my health, sustain my life, and to abolish or alleviated pain or distress be provided to me. Nutrition and hydration shall not be withheld or withdrawn from me if I would die from malnutrition or dehydration rather than from my injury, disease, illness or condition.

    ☐   If at any time I should become unable to communicate my instructions and where the application of artificial life-sustaining procedures shall serve only to prolong artificially the moment of my death, I direct such procedures be withheld or withdrawn except for the administration of nutrition and hydration.

    ☐   If at any time I should become unable to communicate my instructions and where the application of artificial life-sustaining procedures shall serve only to prolong artificially the moment of death, I direct such procedures be withheld or withdrawn including withdrawal of the administration of nutrition and hydration.

2.   In the absence of my ability to give directions regarding the use of life-sustaining proce-dures, I hereby appoint _____ (name) currently residing at

_____, as my attorney-in-fact/proxy for the making of decisions relating to my health care in my place; and it is my intention that this appointment shall be honored by him/her, by my family, relatives, friends, physi-cians and lawyer as the final expression of my legal right to refuse medical or surgical treatment; and I accept the consequences of such a decision. I have duly executed a Durable Power of Attorney for health care decisions on this date.

3.   In the absence of my ability to give further directions regarding my treatment, including life-sustaining procedures, it is my intention that this directive shall be honored by my family and physicians as the final expression of my legal right to refuse or accept medical and surgical treatment, and I accept the consequences of such refusal.

4.   If I have been diagnosed as pregnant and that diagnosis is known to any interested person, this directive shall have no force during the course of my pregnancy.

5.   I understand the full importance of this directive and am emotionally and mentally com-petent to make this directive. No participant in the making of this directive or in its being carried into effect, whether it be a medical doctor, my spouse, a relative, friend or any other person shall be held responsible in any way, legally, professionally or socially, for complying with my directions.

Signed_____

City, county and state of residence _____

The declarant has been known to me personally and I believe him/her to be of sound mind.

Witness _____   Witness _____

Address _____   Address _____

_____   _____

DECLARATION

This declaration is made this _____ day of _____ (month, year). I, _____, being of sound mind, willfully and voluntarily make known my desires that my moment of death shall not be artificially postponed.

If at any time I should have an incurable and irreversible injury, disease, or illness judged to be a terminal condition by my attending physician who has personally examined me and has determined that my death is imminent except for death delaying procedures, I direct that such procedures which would only prolong the dying process be withheld or withdrawn, and that I be permitted to die naturally with only the administration of medication, sustenance, or the performance of any medical procedure deemed necessary by my attending physician to provide me with comfort care.

In the absence of my ability to give directions regarding the use of such death delaying procedures, it is my intention that this declaration shall be honored by my family and physician as the final expression of my legal right to refuse medical or surgical treatment and accept the consequences from such refusal.

Signed _____

City, County and State of Residence _____

The declarant is personally known to me and I believe him or her to be of sound mind. I saw the declarant sign the declaration in my presence (or the declarant acknowledged in my presence that he or she had signed the declaration) and I signed the declaration as a witness in the presence of the declarant. I did not sign the declarant's signature above for or at the direction of the declarant. At the date of this instrument, I am not entitled to any portion of the estate of the declarant according to the laws of intestate succession or, to the best of my knowledge and belief, under any will or declarant or other instrument taking effect at declarant's death, or directly financially responsible for declarant's medical care.

Witness _____

Witness _____

LIVING WILL DECLARATION

Declaration made this _____ day of _____ (month, year).

I, _____, being at least eighteen (18) years of age and of sound mind, willfully, and voluntarily make known my desires that my dying shall not be artificially prolonged under the circumstances set forth below, and I declare:

If at any time my attending physician certifies in writing that: (1) I have an incurable injury, disease, or illness; (2) my death will occur within a short time; and (3) the use of life prolonging procedures would serve only to artificially prolong the dying process, I direct that such procedures be withheld or withdrawn, and that I be permitted to die naturally with only the performance or provision of any medical procedure or medication necessary to provide me with comfort care or to alleviate pain, and, if I have so indicated below, the provision of artificially supplied nutrition and hydration. (Indicate your choice by initialing or making your mark before signing this declaration):

_____ I wish to receive artificially supplied nutrition and hydration, even if the effort to sustain life is futile or excessively burdensome to me.

_____ I do not wish to receive artificially supplied nutrition and hydration, if the effort to sustain life is futile or excessively burdensome to me.

_____ I intentionally make no decision concerning artificially supplied nutrition and hydration, leaving the decision to my health care representative appointed under IC 16-36-1-7 or my attorney in fact with health care powers under IC 30-5-5.

In the absence of my ability to give directions regarding the use of life prolonging procedures, it is my intention that this declaration be honored by my family and physician as the final expression of my legal right to refuse medical or surgical treatment and accept the consequences of the refusal.

I understand the full import of this declaration.

Signed _____

_____
City, County, and State of Residence

The declarant has been personally known to me, and I believe (him/her) to be of sound mind. I did not sign the declarant's signature above for or at the direction of the declarant. I am not a parent, spouse, or child of the declarant. I am not entitled to any part of the declarant's estate or directly financially responsible for the declarant's medical care. I am competent and at least eighteen (18) years of age.

Witness _____   Date _____

Witness _____   Date _____

LIFE PROLONGING PROCEDURES DECLARATION

Declaration made this _____ day of _____ (month, year). I,_____, being at least eighteen (18) years of age and of sound mind, willfully and voluntarily make known my desire that if at any time I have an incurable injury, disease, or illness determined to be a terminal condition I request the use of life pro-longing procedures that would extend my life. This includes appropriate nutrition and hydration, the administration of medication, and the performance of all other medical procedures necessary to extend my life, to provide comfort care, or to alleviate pain.

In the absence of my ability to give directions regarding the use of life prolonging procedures, it is my intention that this declaration be honored by my family and physician as the final expression of my legal right to request medical or surgical treatment and accept the consequences of the request.

I understand the full import of this declaration.

Signed _____

_____
City, County, and State of Residence

The declarant has been personally known to me, and I believe (him/her) to be of sound mind. I am competent and at least eighteen (18) years of age.

Witness_____ Date_____

Witness _____ Date_____

LIVING WILL

If I should have an incurable or irreversible condition that will result either in death within a relatively short period of time or a state of permanent unconsciousness from which, to a reasonable degree of medical certainty, there can be no recovery, it is my desire that my life not be prolonged by the administration of life-sustaining procedures. If I am unable to participate in my health care decisions, I direct my attending physician to withhold or withdraw life-sustaining procedures that merely prolong the dying process and are not necessary to my comfort or freedom from pain.

Date _____   _____

                                                 Signature

Witness: _____

Witness: _____

DECLARATION

Declaration made this _____ day of _____ (month, year). I, _____, being of sound mind, willfully and voluntarily make known my desire that my dying shall not be artificially prolonged under the circumstances set forth below, do hereby declare:

If at any time I should have an incurable injury, disease, or illness certified to be a terminal condition by two physicians who have personally examined me, one of whom shall be my attending physician, and the physicians have determined that my death will occur whether or not life-sustaining procedures are utilized and where the application of life-sustaining procedures would serve only to artificially prolong the dying process, I direct that such procedures be withheld or withdrawn, and that I be permitted to die naturally with only the administration of medication or the performance of any medical procedure deemed necessary to provide me with comfort care.

In the absence of my ability to give directions regarding the use of such life-sustaining procedures, it is my intention that this declaration shall be honored by my family and physician(s) as the final expression of my legal right to refuse medical or surgical treatment and accept the consequences from such refusal.

I understand the full import of this declaration and I am emotionally and mentally competent to make this declaration.

Signed _____

City, County and State of Residence _____

The declarant has been personally known to me and I believe the declarant to be of sound mind. I did not sign the declarant's signature above for or at the direction of the declarant. I am not related to the declarant by blood or marriage, entitled to any portion of the estate of the declarant according to the laws of intestate succession or under any will of declarant or codicil thereto, or directly financially responsible for declarant's medical care.

Witness _____

Witness _____

(OR)

STATE OF _____)

_____ ss.

COUNTY OF _____)

This instrument was acknowledged before me on _____ (date) by
_____ (name of person)

_____
(Signature of notary public)

(Seal, if any)

My appointment expires: _____

Living Will Directive

My wishes regarding life-prolonging treatment and artificially provided nutrition and hydration to be provided to me if I no longer have decisional capacity, have a terminal condition, or become permanently unconscious have been indicated by checking and initialing the appropriate lines below. By checking and initialing the appropriate lines, I specifically:

_____ Designate _____ as my health care surrogate(s) to make health care decisions for me in accordance with this directive when I no longer have decisional capacity. If _____ refuses or is not able to act for me, I designate _____ as my health care surrogate(s).

Any prior designation is revoked.

If I do not designate a surrogate, the following are my directions to my attending physician. If I have designated a surrogate, my surrogate shall comply with my wishes as indicated below:

_____ Direct that treatment be withheld or withdrawn, and that I be permitted to die naturally with only the administration of medication or the performance of any medical treatment deemed necessary to alleviate pain.

_____ DO NOT authorize that life-prolonging treatment be withheld or withdrawn.

_____ Authorize the withholding or withdrawal of artificially provided food, water, or other artificially provided nourishment or fluids.

_____ DO NOT authorize the withholding or withdrawal of artificially provided food, water, or other artificially provided nourishment or fluids.

_____ Authorize my surrogate, designated above, to withhold or withdraw artificially provided nourishment or fluids, or other treatment if the surrogate determines that withholding or withdrawing is in my best interest; but I do not mandate that withholding or withdrawing.

_____ Authorize the giving of all of any part of my body upon death for any purpose specified in KRS 311.185.

_____ DO NOT authorize the giving of all or any part of my body upon death.

In the absence of my ability to give direction regarding the use of life-prolonging treatment and artificially provided nutrition and hydration, it is my intention that this directive shall be honored by my attending physician, my family, and any surrogate designated pursuant to this directive as the final expression of my legal right to refuse medical or surgical treatment and I accept the consequences of the refusal.

If I have been diagnosed as pregnant and that diagnosis is known to my attending physician, this directive shall have no force or effect during the course of my pregnancy.

I understand the full import of this directive and I am emotionally and mentally competent to make this directive.

Signed this _____ day of _____, 200_____.

_____

Signature

_____

Address

In our joint presence, the grantor, who is of sound mind and eighteen (18) years of age, or older, voluntarily dated and signed this writing or directed it to be dated and signed for the grantor.

_____   _____

Signature of witness   Signature of witness

_____   _____

Address   Address

OR

STATE OF KENTUCKY   )

_____ COUNTY   )

Before me, the undersigned authority, came the grantor who is of sound mind and eighteen (18) years of age, or older, and acknowledged that he voluntarily dated and signed this writing or directed it to be signed and dated as above.

Done this _____ day of _____, 200_____.

_____

Signature of Notary Public or other officer

Date commission expires: _____

Execution of this document restricts withholding and withdrawing of some medical procedures. Consult Kentucky Revised Statutes or your attorney.

DECLARATION

Declaration made this _____ day of _____ (month, year).

I, _____, being of sound mind, willfully and voluntarily make known my desire that my dying shall not be artificially prolonged under the circumstances set forth below and do hereby declare:

If at any time I should have an incurable injury, disease or illness, or be in a continual profound comatose state with no reasonable chance of recovery, certified to be a terminal and irreversible condition by two physicians who have personally examined me, one of whom shall be my attending physician, and the physicians have determined that my death will occur whether or not life-sustaining procedures are utilized and where the application of life-sustaining procedure would serve only to prolong artificially the dying process, I direct that such procedures be withheld or withdrawn and that I be permitted to die naturally with only the administration of medication or the performance of any medical procedure deemed necessary to provide me with comfort care.

In the absence of my ability to give directions regarding the use of such life-sustaining procedures, it is my intention that this declaration shall be honored by my family and physician(s) as the final expression of my legal right to refuse medical or surgical treatment and accept the consequences from such refusal.

I understand the full import of this declaration and I am emotionally and mentally competent to make this declaration.

Signed_____

City, Parish, and State of Residence_____

The declarant has been personally known to me and I believe him or her to be of sound mind.

Witness _____

Witness _____

ADVANCE HEALTH-CARE DIRECTIVE

Explanation

You have the right to give instructions about your own health care. You also have the right to name someone else to make health-care decisions for you. This form lets you do either or both of these things. It also lets you express your wishes regarding donation of organs and the designation of your primary physician. If you use this form, you may complete or modify all or any part of it. You are free to use a different form.

Part 1 of this form is a power of attorney for health care. Part 1 lets you name another individual as agent to make health-care decisions for you if you become incapable of making your own decisions or if you want someone else to make those decisions for you now even though you are still capable. You may also name an alternate agent to act for you if your first choice is not willing, able or reasonably available to make decisions for you. Unless related to you, your agent may not be an owner, operator or employee of a residential long-term health-care institution at which you are receiving care.

Unless the form you sign limits the authority of your agent, your agent may make all health-care decisions for you. This form has a place for you to limit the authority of your agent. You need not limit the authority of your agent if you wish to rely on your agent for all health-care decisions that may have to be made. If you choose not to limit the authority of your agent, your agent will have the right to:

(a) Consent or refuse consent to any care, treatment, service or procedure to maintain, diagnose or otherwise affect a physical or mental condition;

(b) Select or discharge health-care providers and institutions;

(c) Approve or disapprove diagnostic tests, surgical procedures, programs of medication and orders not to resuscitate; and

(d) Direct the provision, withholding or withdrawal of artificial nutrition and hydration and all other forms of health care, including life-sustaining treatment.

Part 2 of this form lets you give specific instructions about any aspect of your health care. Choices are provided for you to express your wishes regarding the provision, withholding or withdrawal of treatment to keep you alive, including the provision of artificial nutrition and hydration, as well as the provision of pain relief. Space is also provided for you to add to the choices you have made or for you to write out any additional wishes.

Part 3 of this form lets you express an intention to donate your bodily organs and tissues following your death.

Part 4 of this form lets you designate a physician to have primary responsibility for your health care.

After completing this form, sign and date the form at the end. You must have 2 other individuals sign as witnesses. Give a copy of the signed and completed form to your physician, to any other health-care providers you may have, to any health-care institution at which you are receiving care and to any health-care agents you have named. You should talk to the person you have named as agent to make sure that he or she understands your wishes and is willing to take the responsibility.

You have the right to revoke this advance health-care directive or replace this form at any time.

* * * * * * * * * * * * * * * * * *

PART 1. POWER OF ATTORNEY FOR HEALTH CARE

(1) DESIGNATION OF AGENT: I designate the following individual as my agent to make health-care decisions for me:

_____
(name of individual you choose as agent)

_____
(address)   (city)   (state)   (zip code)

_____
(home phone)   (work phone)

OPTIONAL: If I revoke my agent's authority or if my agent is not willing, able or reasonably available to make a health-care decision for me, I designate as my first alternate agent:

_____
(name of individual you choose as first alternate agent)

_____
(address)   (city)   (state)   (zip code)

_____
(home phone)   (work phone)

OPTIONAL: If I revoke the authority of my agent and first alternate agent or if neither is willing, able or reasonably available to make a health-care decision for me, I designate as my second alternate agent:

_____
(name of individual you choose as second alternate agent)

_____
(address)   (city)   (state)   (zip code)

_____
(home phone)   (work phone)

(2) AGENT'S AUTHORITY: My agent is authorized to make all health-care decisions for me, including decisions to provide, withhold or withdraw artificial nutrition and hydration and all other forms of health care to keep me alive, except as I state here:

_____
_____
_____
(Add additional sheets if needed)

(3) WHEN AGENT'S AUTHORITY BECOMES EFFECTIVE: My agent's authority becomes effective when my primary physician determines that I am unable to make my own health-care decisions unless I mark the following box. If I mark this box [ ], my agent's authority to make health-care decisions for me takes effect immediately.

(4) AGENT'S OBLIGATION: My agent shall make health-care decisions for me in accordance with this power of attorney for health care, any instructions I give in Part 2 of this form and my other wishes to the extent known to my agent. To the extent my wishes are unknown, my agent shall make health-care decisions for me in accordance with what my agent determines to be in my best interest. In determining my best interest, my agent shall consider my personal values to the extent known to my agent.

(5) NOMINATION OF GUARDIAN: If a guardian of my person needs to be appointed for me by a court, I nominate the agent designated in this form. If that agent is not willing, able or reasonably available to act as guardian, I nominate the alternate agents whom I have named, in the order designated.

PART 2. INSTRUCTIONS FOR HEALTH CARE

If you are satisfied to allow your agent to determine what is best for you in making end-of-life decisions, you need not fill out this part of the form. If you do fill out this part of the form, you may strike any wording you do not want.

(6) END-OF-LIFE DECISIONS: I direct that my health-care providers and others involved in my care provide, withhold or withdraw treatment in accordance with the choice I have marked below:

    [ ] (a) Choice Not To Prolong Life: I do not want my life to be prolonged if (i) I have an incurable and irreversible condition that will result in my death within a relatively short time, (ii) I become unconscious and, to a reasonable degree of medical certainty, I will not regain consciousness, or (iii) the likely risks and burdens of treatment would outweigh the expected benefits, OR

    [ ] (b) Choice To Prolong Life: I want my life to be prolonged as long as possible within the limits of generally accepted health-care standards.

(7) ARTIFICIAL NUTRITION AND HYDRATION: Artificial nutrition and hydration must be provided, withheld or withdrawn in accordance with the choice I have made in paragraph (6) unless I mark the following box. If I mark this box [ ], artificial nutrition and hydration must be provided regardless of my condition and regardless of the choice I have made in paragraph (6).

(8) RELIEF FROM PAIN: Except as I state in the following space, I direct that treatment for alleviation of pain or discomfort be provided at all times, even if it hastens my death: _____

_____

(9) OTHER WISHES: (If you do not agree with any of the optional choices above and wish to write your own, or if you wish to add to the instructions you have given above, you may do so here.) I direct that:_____

_____

_____

(Add additional sheets if needed)

PART 3. DONATION OF ORGANS AT DEATH (OPTIONAL)

(10) Upon my death (mark applicable box)
    [ ] (a) I give needed organs, tissues or parts OR
    [ ] (b) I give the following organs, tissues or parts only

        _____

    [ ] (c) My gift is for the following purposes (strike any of the following you do not want)
        (i)   Transplant
        (ii)   Therapy
        (iii)   Research
        (iv)   Education

PART 4. PRIMARY PHYSICIAN (OPTIONAL)

(11) I designate the following physician as my primary physician:

_____

        (name of physician)   (phone)

_____

    (address)   (city)   (state)   (zip code)

OPTIONAL: If the physician I have designated above is not willing, able or reasonably available to act as my primary physician, I designate the following physician as my primary physician:

_____

        (name of physician)   (phone)

_____

    (address)   (city)   (state)   (zip code)

* * * * * * * * * * * * * * * * * * *

(12)   EFFECT OF COPY: A copy of this form has the same effect as the original.

(13)   SIGNATURES: Sign and date the form here:

_____   _____
(date)   (sign your name)

_____   _____
(address)   (print your name)

_____
(city)   (state)

SIGNATURES OF WITNESSES:

          First witness   Second witness

_____   _____
(print name)   (print name)

_____   _____
(address)   (address)

_____   _____
(city   (state)   (city)   (state)

_____   _____
(signature of witness)   (signature of witness)

_____   _____
(date)   (date)

HEALTH CARE DECISION MAKING FORMS

The following form allows you to make some decisions about future health care issues. The form, called a "living will," allows you to make decisions about life-sustaining procedures if, in the future, your death from a terminal condition is imminent despite the application of life-sustaining procedures or you are in a persistent vegetative state.

This form is intended to be a guide. You may complete all or only part of the form that you use. Different forms may also be used.

Please note: If you decide to select a health care agent that person may not be a witness to your advance directive. Also, at least one of your witnesses may not be a person who may financially benefit by reason of your death.

Living Will
(Optional Form)

If I am not able to make an informed decision regarding my health care, I direct my health care providers to follow my instructions as set forth below. (Initial those statements you wish to be included in the document and cross through those statements which do not apply.)

a.   If my death from a terminal condition is imminent and even if life-sustaining procedures are used there is no reasonable expectation of my recovery —

_____ I direct that my life not be extended by life-sustaining procedures, including the administration of nutrition and hydration artificially.

_____ I direct that my life not be extended by life-sustaining procedures, except that, if I am unable to take food by mouth, I wish to receive nutrition and hydration artificially.

_____ I direct that, even in a terminal condition, I be given all available medical treatment in accordance with accepted health care standards.

b.   If I am in a persistent vegetative state, that is if I am not conscious and am not aware of my environment nor able to interact with others, and there is no reasonable expectation of my recovery within a medically appropriate period —

_____ I direct that my life not be extended by life-sustaining procedures, including the administration of nutrition and hydration artificially.

_____ I direct that my life not be extended by life-sustaining procedures, except that, if I am unable to take food by mouth, I wish to receive nutrition and hydration artificially.

_____ I direct that I be given all available medical treatment in accordance with accepted health care standards.

c. If I am pregnant my health care providers shall follow these specific instructions:

_____
_____
_____

d. Upon my death, I wish to donate:

_____ Any needed organs, tissue, or eyes.
_____ Only the following organs, tissues, or eyes: _____
_____

I authorize the use of my organs, tissues, or eyes:
_____ For transplantation
_____ For therapy
_____ For research
_____ For medical education
_____ For any purpose authorized by law

I understand that before any vital organ, tissue, or eye may be removed for transplantation, I must be pronounced dead. After death, I direct that all support measures be continued to maintain the viability for transplantation of my organs, tissue, and eyes until organ, tissue, and eye recovery has been completed.

I understand that my estate will not be charged for any costs associated with my decision to donate my organs, tissue, or eyes or the actual disposition of my organs, tissue, or eyes.

By signing below, I indicate that I am emotionally and mentally competent to make this living will and that I understand its purpose and effect.

_____   _____
(Date)   (Signature of Declarant)

The declarant signed or acknowledged signing this living will in my presence and based upon my personal observation the declarant appears to be a competent individual.

_____   _____
(Witness)   (Witness)
              (Signature of Two Witnesses)

HEALTH CARE LIVING WILL

Notice:

This is an important legal document. Before signing this document, you should know these important facts:

(a) This document gives your health care providers or your designated proxy the power and guidance to make health care decisions according to your wishes when you are in a terminal condition and cannot do so. This document may include what kind of treatment you want or do not want and under what circumstances you want these decisions to be made. You may state where you want or do not want to receive any treatment.

(b) If you name a proxy in this document and that person agrees to serve as your proxy, that person has a duty to act consistently with your wishes. If the proxy does not know your wishes, the proxy has the duty to act in your best interests. If you do not name a proxy, your health care providers have a duty to act consistently with your instructions or tell you that they are unwilling to do so.

(c) This document will remain valid and in effect until and unless you amend or revoke it. Review this document periodically to make sure it continues to reflect your preferences. You may amend or revoke the living will at any time by notifying your health care providers.

(d) Your named proxy has the same right as you have to examine your medical records and to consent to their disclosure for purposes related to your health care or insurance unless you limit this right in this document.

(e) If there is anything in this document that you do not understand, you should ask for professional help to have it explained to you.

TO MY FAMILY, DOCTORS, AND ALL THOSE CONCERNED WITH MY CARE:

I, _____ , born on _____ , 19_____ (birthdate), being an adult of sound mind, willfully and voluntarily make this statement as a directive to be followed if I am in a terminal condition and become unable to participate in decisions regarding my health care. I understand that my health care providers are legally bound to act consistently with my wishes, within the limits of reasonable medical practice and other applicable law. I also understand that I have the right to make medical and health care decisions for myself as long as I am able to do so and to revoke this living will at any time.

(1) The following are my feelings and wishes regarding my health care (you may state the circumstances under which this living will applies):

_____
_____
_____
_____

(2) I particularly want to have all appropriate health care that will help in the following ways (you may give instructions for care you do want):

_____
_____
_____
_____

(3) I particularly do not want the following (you may list specific treatment you do not want in certain circumstances):

_____
_____
_____
_____

(4) I particularly want to have the following kinds of life-sustaining treatment if I am diagnosed to have a terminal condition (you may list the specific types of life-sustaining treatment that you do want if you have a terminal condition):

_____
_____
_____

(5) I particularly do not want the following kinds of life-sustaining treatment if I am diagnosed to have a terminal condition (you may list the specific types of life-sustaining treatment that you do not want if you have a terminal condition):

_____
_____
_____

(6) I recognize that if I reject artificially administered sustenance, then I may die of dehydration or malnutrition rather than from my illness or injury. The following are my feelings and wishes regarding artificially administered sustenance should I have a terminal condition (you may indicate whether you wish to receive food and fluids given to you in some other way than be mouth if you have a terminal condition):

_____
_____
_____

(7) Thoughts I feel are relevant to my instructions. (You may, but need not, give your religious beliefs, philosophy, or other personal values that you feel are important. You may also state preferences concerning the location of your care.):

_____
_____
_____

(8) **Proxy Designation.** (If you wish, you may name someone to see that your wishes are carried out, but you do not have to do this. You may also name a proxy without including specific instructions regarding your care. If you name a proxy, you should discuss your wishes with that person.)

If I become unable to communicate my instructions, I designate the following person(s) to act on my behalf consistently with my instructions, if any, as stated in this document. Unless I write instructions that limit my proxy's authority, my proxy has full power and authority to make health care decisions for me. If a guardian or conservator of the person is to be appointed for me, I nominate my proxy named in this document to act as guardian or conservator of my person.

Name:_____
Address:_____
Phone Number:_____
Relationship: (If any) _____

If the person I have named above refuses or is unable or unavailable to act on my behalf, or if I revoke that person's authority to act as my proxy, I authorize the following person to do so:

Name:_____
Address:_____
Phone Number:_____
Relationship: (If any) _____

I understand that I have the right to revoke the appointment of the persons named above to act on my behalf at any time by communicating that decision to the proxy or my health care provider.

(9) **Organ Donation After Death.** (If you wish, you may indicate whether you want to be an organ donor upon your death.) Initial the statement which expresses your wish:

_____ In the event of my death, I would like to donate my organs. I understand that to become an organ donor, I must be declared brain dead. My organ function may be maintained artificially on a breathing machine, (i.e., artificial ventilation), so that my organs can be removed.

Limitations or special wishes: (If any) _____
_____
_____

I understand that, upon my death, my next of kin may be asked permission for donation. Therefore, it is in my best interests to inform my next of kin about my decision ahead of time and ask them to honor my request.
I (have) (have not) agreed in another document or on another form to donate some or all of my organs when I die.

_____ I do not wish to become an organ donor upon my death.

DATE: _____   SIGNED: _____

STATE OF _____

COUNTY OF _____

Subscribed, sworn to, and acknowledged before me by _____ on this _____ day of _____, 200____.

_____
NOTARY PUBLIC

OR

(Sign and date here in the presence of two adult witnesses, neither of whom is entitled to any part of your estate under a will or by operation of law, and neither of whom is your proxy.)
I certify that the declarant voluntarily signed this living will in my presence and that the declarant is personally known to me. I am not named as a proxy by the living will, and to the best of my knowledge, I am not entitled to any part of the estate of the declarant under a will or by operation of law.

Witness _____   Address _____

_____

Witness _____   Address _____

_____

Reminder: Keep the signed original with your personal papers.
Give signed copies to your doctor, family, and proxy.

ADVANCE HEALTH-CARE DIRECTIVE

Explanation

You have the right to give instructions about your own health care. You also have the right to name someone else to make health-care decisions for you. This form lets you do either or both of these things. It also lets you express your wishes regarding the designation of your primary physician. If you use this form you may complete or modify all or any part of it. You are free to use a different form.

Part 1 of this form is a power of attorney for health care. Part 1 lets you name another individual as agent to make health-care decisions for you if you become incapable of making your own decisions or if you want someone else to make those decisions for you now even though you are still capable. You may name an alternate agent to act for you if your first choice is not willing, able, or reasonably available to make decisions for you. Unless related to you, your agent may not be an owner, operator, or employee of a residential long-term health-care institution at which you are receiving care.

Unless the form you sign limits the authority of your agent, your agent may make all health-care decisions for you. This form has a place for you to limit the authority of your agent. You need not limit the authority of your agent if you wish to rely on your agent for all health-care decisions that may have to be made. If you choose not to limit the authority of your agent, your agent will have the right to:

(a) Consent or refuse consent to any care, treatment, service, or procedure to maintain, diagnose, or otherwise affect a physical or mental condition;

(b) Select or discharge health-care providers and institutions;

(c) Approve or disapprove diagnostic tests, surgical procedures, programs of medication, and orders not to resuscitate; and

(d) Direct the provision, withholding, or withdrawal of artificial nutrition and hydration and all other forms of health care, including life-sustaining treatment.

Part 2 of this form lets you give specific instructions about any aspect of your health care. Choices are provided for you to express your wishes regarding the provision, withholding, or withdrawal of treatment to keep you alive, including the provision of artificial nutrition and hydration, as well as the provision of pain relief. Space is also provided for you to add to the choices you have made or for you to write out any additional wishes.

Part 3 of this form lets you designate a physician to have primary responsibility for your health care.

After completing this form, sign and date the form at the end and have the form witnessed by one of the two alternative methods listed below. Give a copy of the signed and completed form to your physician, to any other health-care providers you may have, to any health-care institution at which you are receiving care, and to any health-care agents you have named. You should talk to the person you have named as agent to make sure that he or she understands your wishes and is willing to take the responsibility.

You have the right to revoke this advance health-care directive or replace this form at any time.

* * * * * * * * * * * * * * * * * *

PART 1. POWER OF ATTORNEY FOR HEALTH CARE

(1) DESIGNATION OF AGENT: I designate the following individual as my agent to make health-care decisions for me:

_____
(name of individual you choose as agent)

_____
(address)   (city)   (state)   (zip code)

_____
(home phone)   (work phone)

OPTIONAL: If I revoke my agent's authority or if my agent is not willing, able, or reasonably available to make a health-care decision for me, I designate as my first alternate agent:

_____
(name of individual you choose as first alternate agent)

_____
(address)   (city)   (state)   (zip code)

_____
(home phone)   (work phone)

OPTIONAL: If I revoke the authority of my agent and first alternate agent or if neither is willing, able or reasonably available to make a health-care decision for me, I designate as my second alternate agent:

_____
(name of individual you choose as second alternate agent)

_____
(address)   (city)   (state)   (zip code)

_____
(home phone)   (work phone)

(2) AGENT'S AUTHORITY: My agent is authorized to make all health-care decisions for me, including decisions to provide, withhold, or withdraw artificial nutrition and hydration and all other forms of health care to keep me alive, except as I state here:

_____
_____
_____
(Add additional sheets if needed)

(3) WHEN AGENT'S AUTHORITY BECOMES EFFECTIVE: My agent's authority becomes effective when my primary physician determines that I am unable to make my own health-care decisions, unless I mark the following box. If I mark this box [ ], my agent's authority to make health-care decisions for me takes effect immediately.

(4) AGENT'S OBLIGATION: My agent shall make health-care decisions for me in accordance with this power of attorney for health care, any instructions I give in Part 2 of this form, and my other wishes to the extent known to my agent. To the extent my wishes are unknown, my agent shall make health-care decisions for me in accordance with what my agent determines to be in my best interest. In determining my best interest, my agent shall consider my personal values to the extent known to my agent.

(5) NOMINATION OF GUARDIAN: If a guardian of my person needs to be appointed for me by a court, I nominate the agent designated in this form. If that agent is not willing, able or reasonably available to act as guardian, I nominate the alternate agents whom I have named, in the order designated.

PART 2. INSTRUCTIONS FOR HEALTH CARE

If you are satisfied to allow your agent to determine what is best for you in making end-of-life decisions, you need not fill out this part of the form. If you do fill out this part of the form, you may strike any wording you do not want.

(6) END-OF-LIFE DECISIONS: I direct that my health-care providers and others involved in my care provide, withhold, or withdraw treatment in accordance with the choice I have marked below:

[ ] (a) Choice Not To Prolong Life: I do not want my life to be prolonged if (i) I have an incurable and irreversible condition that will result in my death within a relatively short time, (ii) I become unconscious and, to a reasonable degree of medical certainty, I will not regain consciousness, or (iii) the likely risks and burdens of treatment would outweigh the expected benefits, OR

[ ] (b) Choice To Prolong Life: I want my life to be prolonged as long as possible within the limits of generally accepted health-care standards.

(7) ARTIFICIAL NUTRITION AND HYDRATION: Artificial nutrition and hydration must be provided, withheld, or withdrawn in accordance with the choice I have made in paragraph (6) unless I mark the following box. If I mark this box [ ], artificial nutrition and hydration must be provided regardless of my condition and regardless of the choice I have made in paragraph (6).

(8) RELIEF FROM PAIN: Except as I state in the following space, I direct that treatment for alleviation of pain or discomfort be provided at all times, even if it hastens my death: _____

_____

(9) OTHER WISHES: (If you do not agree with any of the optional choices above and wish to write your own, or if you wish to add to the instructions you have given above, you may do so here.) I direct that: _____

_____

(Add additional sheets if needed)

PART 3. PRIMARY PHYSICIAN (OPTIONAL)

(10) I designate the following physician as my primary physician:

_____   _____
(name of physician)   (phone)

_____
(address)   (city)   (state)   (zip code)

OPTIONAL: If the physician I have designated above is not willing, able or reasonably available to act as my primary physician, I designate the following physician as my primary physician:

_____   _____
(name of physician)   (phone)

_____
(address)   (city)   (state)   (zip code)

* * * * * * * * * * * * * * * * * *

(11) EFFECT OF COPY: A copy of this form has the same effect as the original.

(12) SIGNATURES: Sign and date the form here:

_____   _____
(date)   (sign your name)

_____   _____
(address)   (print your name)

_____
(city)   (state)

(13)   WITNESSES: This power of attorney will not be valid for making health-care decisions unless it is either (a) signed by two (2) qualified adult witnesses who are personally know you you and who are present when you sign or acknowledge your signature; or (b) acknowledged before a notary public in the state.

ALTERNATIVE NO. 1
Witnesses

I declare under penalty of perjury, pursuant to Section 97-9-61, Mississippi Code of 1972, that the principal is personally known to me, that the principal signed or acknowledged this power of attorney in my presence, that the principal appears to be of sound mine and under no duress, fraud, or undue influence; that I am not the person appointed as agent by this document; and that I am not a health-care provider nor an employee of a health-care provider or facility. I am not related to the principal by blood, marriage, or adoption; and to the best of my knowledge I am not entitled to any part of the estate of the principal upon the death of the principal under a will now existing or by operation of law.

_____	_____
(date)	(signature of witness)
_____	_____
(address)	(printed name of witness)
_____	
(city) (state)	

I declare under penalty of perjury, pursuant to Section 97-9-61, Mississippi Code of 1972, that the principal is personally known to me, that the principal signed or acknowledged this power of attorney in my presence, that the principal appears to be of sound mine and under no duress, fraud, or undue influence; that I am not the person appointed as agent by this document; and that I am not a health-care provider nor an employee of a health-care provider or facility.

_____	_____
(date)	(signature of witness)
_____	_____
(address)	(printed name of witness)
_____	
(city) (state)	

ALTERNATIVE NO. 2

State of _____

County of _____

On this _____ day of _____, in the year 200___, before me, _____ _____ (insert name of notary public), appeared _____ _____, personally known to me (or proved to me on the basis of satisfactory evidence) to be the person whose name is subscribed to this instrument and acknowledged that he or she executed it. I declare under the penalty of perjury that the person whose name is subscribed to this instrument appears to be of sound mind and under no duress, fraud, or undue influence.

Notary Seal

_____
(Signature of Notary public)

DECLARATION

I have the primary right to make my own decisions concerning treatment that might unduly prolong the dying process. By this declaration I express to my physician, family and friends my intent. If I should have a terminal condition it is my desire that my dying not be prolonged by administration of death-prolonging procedures. If my condition is terminal and I am unable to participate in decisions regarding my medical treatment, I direct my attending physician to withhold or withdraw medical procedures that merely prolong the dying process and are not necessary to my comfort or to alleviate pain. It is not my intent to authorize affirmative or deliberate acts or omissions to shorten my life rather only to permit the natural process of dying.

Signed this _____ day of _____, 200_____.

Signature _____

City, County and State of residence _____

The declarant is known to me, is eighteen years of age or older, of sound mind and voluntarily signed this document in my presence.

Witness_____
Address_____
_____

Witness_____
Address_____
_____

REVOCATION PROVISION

I hereby revoke the above declaration,

Signed _____
(Signature of Declarant)

Date _____

Directive to Physicians

If I should have an incurable or irreversible condition that, without the administration of life-sustaining treatment, will, in the opinion of my attending physician, cause my death within a relatively short time and I am no longer able to make decisions regarding my medical treatment, I direct my attending physician, pursuant to the Montana Rights of the Terminally Ill Act, to withhold or withdraw treatment that only prolongs the process of dying and is not necessary to my comfort or to alleviate pain.

Signed this _____ day of _____, 200____.

Signature _____

City, County, and State of Residence _____

The declarant voluntarily signed this document in my presence.

Witness_____

Address _____

Witness_____

Address _____

DECLARATION

If I should have an incurable and irreversible condition that, without the administration of life-sustaining treatment, will, in the opinion of my attending physician or attending advanced practice registered nurse, cause my death within a relatively short time and I am no longer able to make decisions regarding my medical treatment, I appoint _____ or, if he or she is not reasonably available or is unwilling to serve, _____, to make decisions on my behalf regarding withholding or withdrawal of treatment that only prolongs the process of dying and is not necessary for my comfort or to alleviate pain, pursuant to the Montana Rights of the Terminally Ill Act.

If the individual I have appointed is not reasonably available or is unwilling to serve, I direct my attending physician or attending advanced practice registered nurse, pursuant to the Montana Rights of the Terminally Ill Act, to withhold or withdraw treatment that only prolongs the process of dying and is not necessary for my comfort or to alleviate pain.

Signed this _____ day of _____, _____.
Signature _____
City, County, and State of Residence _____

The declarant voluntarily signed this document in my presence.
Witness _____
Address _____
Witness _____
Address _____

Name and address of designee.
Name _____
Address _____

DECLARATION

If I should lapse into a persistent vegetative state or have an incurable and irreversible condition that, without the administration of life-sustaining treatment, will, in the opinion of my attending physician, cause my death within a relatively short time and I am no longer able to make decisions regarding my medical treatment, I direct my attending physician, pursuant to the Rights of the Terminally Ill Act, to withhold or withdraw life sustaining treatment that is not necessary for my comfort or to alleviate pain.

Signed this _____ day of _____.

Signature _____

Address _____

_____

The declarant voluntarily signed this writing in my presence.

_____   _____

Witness   Witness

_____   _____

Address   Address

_____   _____

Or

The declarant voluntarily signed this writing in my presence.

_____

Notary Public

POWER OF ATTORNEY FOR HEALTH CARE

I appoint _____, whose address is _____,
and whose telephone number is _____, as my attorney in fact for health care. I appoint
_____, whose address is _____, and whose
telephone number is _____, as my successor attorney in fact for health care. I authorize my
attorney in fact appointed by this document to make health care decisions for me when I am determined to be incapable of making my own health care decisions. I have read the warning which
accompanies this document and understand the consequences of executing a power of attorney for
health care. I direct that my attorney in fact comply with the following instructions or limitations:
_____.

I direct that my attorney in fact comply with the following instructions on life-sustaining treatment:
(optional) _____.

I direct that my attorney in fact comply with the following instructions on artificially administered
nutrition and hydration: (optional) _____.

I HAVE READ THIS POWER OF ATTORNEY FOR HEALTH CARE. I UNDERSTAND
THAT IT ALLOWS ANOTHER PERSON TO MAKE LIFE AND DEATH DECISIONS FOR
ME IF I AM INCAPABLE OF MAKING SUCH DECISIONS. I ALSO UNDERSTAND THAT
I CAN REVOKE THIS POWER OF ATTORNEY FOR HEALTH CARE AT ANY TIME BY
NOTIFYING MY ATTORNEY IN FACT, MY PHYSICIAN, OR THE FACILITY IN WHICH I
AM A PATIENT OR RESIDENT. I ALSO UNDERSTAND THAT I CAN REQUIRE IN THIS
POWER OF ATTORNEY FOR HEALTH CARE THAT THE FACT OF MY INCAPACITY IN
THE FUTURE BE CONFIRMED BY A SECOND PHYSICIAN.

_____ (Signature of person making designation/date)

DECLARATION OF WITNESSES

We declare that the principal is personally known to us, that the principal signed or acknowledged
his or her signature on this power of attorney for health care in our presence, that the principal
appears to be of sound mind and not under duress or undue influence, and that neither of us nor the
principal's attending physician is the person appointed as attorney in fact by this document.

Witnessed By:

_____   _____
(Signature of Witness/Date):   (Printed Name of Witness):

_____   _____
(Signature of Witness/Date):   (Printed Name of Witness):

OR

State of Nebraska,
County of _____

On this _____ day of _____, 20___, before me, _____, a
notary public in and for _____ County, personally came _____,
personally to me known to be the identical person whose name is affixed to the above power of attorney for health care as principal, and I declare that he or she appears in sound mind and not under
duress or undue influence, that he or she acknowledges the execution of the same to be his or her voluntary act and deed, and that I am not the attorney in fact or successor attorney in fact designated
by this power of attorney for health care. Witness my hand and notarial seal at _____
in such county the day and year last above written.

_____   Seal
Signature of Notary Public

DECLARATION

If I should have an incurable and irreversible condition that, without the administration of life-sustaining treatment, will, in the opinion of my attending physician, cause my death within a relatively short time, and I am no longer able to make decisions regarding my medical treatment, I appoint _____ or, if he or she is not reasonably available or is unwilling to serve, _____, to make decisions on my behalf regarding withholding or withdrawal of treatment that only prolongs the process of dying and is not necessary for my comfort or to alleviate pain, pursuant to NRS 449.535 to 449.690, inclusive. (If the person or persons I have so appointed are not reasonably available or are unwilling to serve, I direct my attending physician, pursuant to those sections, to withhold or withdraw treatment that only prolongs the process of dying and is not necessary for my comfort or to alleviate pain.) Strike language in parentheses if you do not desire it.

If you wish to include this statement in this declaration, you must INITIAL the statement in the box provided:

Withholding or withdrawal of artificial nutrition and hydration may result in death by starvation or dehydration. Initial this box if you want to receive or continue receiving artificial nutrition and hydration by way of the gastro-intestinal tract after all other treatment is withheld pursuant to this declaration. (   )

Signed this _____ day of _____,_____.
Signature   _____
Address   _____

The declarant voluntarily signed this writing in my presence.
Witness   _____
Address   _____
Witness   _____
Address   _____

Name and address of each designee.
Name   _____
Address _____

DECLARATION

Declaration made this _____ day of _____ (month, year). I, _____, being of sound mind, willfully and voluntarily make known my desire that my dying shall not be artificially prolonged under the circumstances set forth below, do hereby declare:

If at any time I should have an incurable injury, disease, or illness certified to be a terminal condition or a permanently unconscious condition by 2 physicians who have personally examined me, one of whom shall be my attending physician, and the physicians have determined that my death will occur whether or not life-sustaining procedures are utilized or that I will remain in a permanently unconscious condition and where the application of life-sustaining procedures would serve only to artificially prolong the dying process, I direct that such procedures be withheld or withdrawn, and that I be permitted to die naturally with only the administration of medication, sustenance, or the performance of any medical procedure deemed necessary to provide me with comfort care. I realize that situations could arise in which the only way to allow me to die would be to discontinue artificial nutrition and hydration. In carrying out any instruction I have given under this section, I authorize that artificial nutrition and hydration not be started or, if started, be discontinued.

(yes) (no) (Circle your choice and initial beneath it. If you choose "yes," artificial nutrition and _____ hydration will be provided and will not be removed.)

In the absence of my ability to give directions regarding the use of such life-sustaining procedures, it is my intention that this declaration shall be honored by my family and physicians as the final expression of my right to refuse medical or surgical treatment and accept the consequences of such refusal.

I understand the full import of this declaration, and I am emotionally and mentally competent to make this declaration.

Signed_____

State of _____
_____County

We, the following witnesses, being duly sworn each declare to the notary public or justice of the peace or other official signing below as follows:

1. The declarant signed the instrument as a free and voluntary act for the purposes expressed, or expressly directed another to sign for him.
2. Each witness signed at the request of the declarant, in his presence, and in the presence of the other witness.
3. To the best of my knowledge, at the time of the signing the declarant was at least 18 years of age, and was of sane mind and under no constraint or undue influence.

_____ Witness
_____ Witness

Sworn to and signed before me by _____, declarant, _____ and _____, witnesses on _____.

_____
Signature

_____
Official Capacity

OPTIONAL ADVANCE HEALTH-CARE DIRECTIVE

Explanation

You have the right to give instructions about your own health care. You also have the right to name someone else to make health-care decisions for you. This form lets you do either or both of these things. It also lets you express your wishes regarding the designation of your primary physician.

THIS FORM IS OPTIONAL. Each paragraph and word of this form is also optional. If you use this form, you may cross out, complete or modify all or any part of it. You are free to use a different form. If you use this form, be sure to sign it and date it.

PART 1 of this form is a power of attorney for health care. PART 1 lets you name another individual as agent to make health-care decisions for you if you become incapable of making your own decisions or if you want someone else to make those decisions for you now even though you are still capable. You may also name an alternate agent to act for you if your first choice is not willing, able or reasonably available to make decisions for you. Unless related to you, your agent may not be an owner, operator or employee of a health care institution at which you are receiving care.

Unless the form you sign limits the authority of your agent, your agent may make all health-care decisions for you. This form has a place for you to limit the authority of your agent. You need not limit the authority of your agent if you wish to rely on your agent for all health-care decisions that may have to be made. If you choose not to limit the authority of your agent, your agent will have the right to:

(a) consent or refuse consent to any care, treatment, service or procedure to maintain, diagnose or otherwise affect a physical or mental condition;

(b) select or discharge health-care providers and institutions;

(c) approve or disapprove diagnostic tests, surgical procedures, programs of medication and orders not to resuscitate; and

(d) direct the provision, withholding or withdrawal of artificial nutrition and hydration and all other forms of health care.

PART 2 of this form lets you give specific instructions about any aspect of your health care. Choices are provided for you to express your wishes regarding life-sustaining treatment, including the provision of artificial nutrition and hydration, as well as the provision of pain relief. In addition, you may express your wishes regarding whether you want to make an anatomical gift of some or all of your organs and tissue. Space is also provided for you to add to the choices you have made or for you to write out any additional wishes.

PART 3 of this form lets you designate a physician to have primary responsibility for your health care.

After completing this form, sign and date the form at the end. It is recommended but not required that you request two other individuals to sign as witnesses. Give a copy of the signed and completed form to your physician, to any other health-care providers you may have, to any health-care institution at which you are receiving care and to any health-care agents you have named. You should talk to the person you have named as agent to make sure that he or she understands your wishes and is willing to take the responsibility.

You have the right to revoke this advance health-care directive or replace this form at any time.

* * * * * * * * * * * * * * * * * *

PART 1. POWER OF ATTORNEY FOR HEALTH CARE

(1) DESIGNATION OF AGENT: I designate the following individual as my agent to make health-care decisions for me:

_____
(name of individual you choose as agent)

_____
(address)   (city)   (state)   (zip code)

_____
(home phone)   (work phone)

If I revoke my agent's authority or if my agent is not willing, able or reasonably available to make a health-care decision for me, I designate as my first alternate agent:

_____
(name of individual you choose as first alternate agent)

_____
(address)   (city)   (state)   (zip code)

_____
(home phone)   (work phone)

If I revoke the authority of my agent and first alternate agent or if neither is willing, able or reasonably available to make a health-care decision for me, I designate as my second alternate agent:

_____
(name of individual you choose as second alternate agent)

_____
(address)   (city)   (state)   (zip code)

_____
(home phone)   (work phone)

(2) AGENT'S AUTHORITY: My agent is authorized to obtain and review medical records, reports and information about me and to make all health-care decisions for me, including decisions to provide, withhold or withdraw artificial nutrition, hydration and all other forms of health care to keep me alive, except as I state here:

_____
_____
_____
(Add additional sheets if needed)

(3) WHEN AGENT'S AUTHORITY BECOMES EFFECTIVE: My agent's authority becomes effective when my primary physician and one other qualified health-care professional determine that I am unable to make my own health-care decisions. If I initial this box [   ], my agent's authority to make health-care decisions for me takes effect immediately.

(4) AGENT'S OBLIGATIONS: My agent shall make health-care decisions for me in accordance with this power of attorney for health care, any instructions I give in Part 2 of this form and my other wishes to the extent known to my agent. To the extent my wishes are unknown, my agent shall make health-care decisions for me in accordance with what my agent determines to be in my best interest. In determining my best interest, my agent shall consider my personal values to the extent known to my agent.

(5) NOMINATION OF GUARDIAN: If a guardian of my person needs to be appointed for me by a court, I nominate the agent designated in this form. If that agent is not willing, able or reasonably available to act as guardian, I nominate the alternate agents whom I have named, in the order designated.

PART 2. INSTRUCTIONS FOR HEALTH CARE

If you are satisfied to allow your agent to determine what is best for you in making end-of-life decisions, you need not fill out this part of the form. If you do fill out this part of the form, you may cross out any wording you do not want.

(6) END-OF-LIFE DECISIONS: If I am unable to make or communicate decisions regarding my health care, and IF (i) I have an incurable or irreversible condition that will result in my death within a relatively short time, OR (ii) I become unconscious and, to a reasonable degree of medical certainty, I will not regain consciousness, OR (iii) the likely risks and burdens of treatment would outweigh the expected benefits, THEN I direct that my health-care providers and others involved in my care provide, withhold or withdraw treatment in accordance with the choice I have initialed below in one of the following three boxes:

[   ]   (a)   I CHOOSE NOT To Prolong Life
I do not want my life to be prolonged.

[   ]   (b)   I CHOOSE To Prolong Life
I want my life to be prolonged as long as possible within the limits of
generally accepted health-care standards.

[   ]   (c)   I CHOOSE To Let My Agent Decide
My agent under my power of attorney for health care may make
life-sustaining treatment decisions for me.

(7) ARTIFICIAL NUTRITION AND HYDRATION: If I have chosen above NOT to prolong life, I also specify by marking my initials below:

[   ]   I DO NOT want artificial nutrition OR

[   ]   I DO want artificial nutrition.

[   ]   I DO NOT want artificial hydration unless required for my comfort OR

[   ]   I DO want artificial hydration.

(8) RELIEF FROM PAIN: Regardless of the choices I have made in this form and except as I state in the following space, I direct that the best medical care possible to keep me clean, comfortable and free of pain or discomfort be provided at all times so that my dignity is maintained, even if this care hastens my death:_____
_____
_____
_____

(9) ANATOMICAL GIFT DESIGNATION: Upon my death I specify as marked below whether I choose to make an anatomical gift of all or some of my organs or tissue:

[   ]   I CHOOSE to make an anatomical gift of all of my organs or tissue to be determined by medical suitability at the time of death, and artificial support may be maintained long enough for organs to be removed.

[   ]   I CHOOSE to make a partial anatomical gift of some of my organs and tissue as specified below, and artificial support may be maintained long enough for organs to be removed.
_____
_____

[   ]   I REFUSE to make an anatomical gift of any of my organs or tissue.

[   ]   I CHOOSE to let my agent decide.

(10) OTHER WISHES: (If you wish to write your own instructions, or if you wish to add to the instructions you have given above, you may do so here.) I direct that:

_____

_____

(Add additional sheets if needed.)

PART 3. PRIMARY PHYSICIAN

(11) I designate the following physician as my primary physician:

_____

(name of physician)   (phone)

_____

(address)   (city)   (state)   (zip code)

If the physician I have designated above is not willing, able or reasonably available to act as my primary physician, I designate the following physician as my primary physician:

_____

(name of physician)   (phone)

_____

(address)   (city)   (state)   (zip code)

* * * * * * * * * * * * * * * * * * * *

(12) EFFECT OF COPY: A copy of this form has the same effect as the original.

(13) REVOCATION: I understand that I may revoke this OPTIONAL ADVANCE HEALTH-CARE DIREC-TIVE at any time, and that if I revoke it, I should promptly notify my supervising health-care provider and any health-care institution where I am receiving care and any others to whom I have given copies of this power of attorney. I understand that I may revoke the designation of an agent either by a signed writing or by personally informing the supervising health-care provider.

(14) SIGNATURES: Sign and date the form here:

_____   _____
(date)   (sign your name)

_____   _____
(address)   (print your name)

_____   _____
(city)   (state)   (your social security number)

(Optional) SIGNATURE OF WITNESSES:

First witness   Second witness

_____   _____
(print name)   (print name)

_____   _____
(address)   (address)

_____   _____
(city)   (state)   (city)   (state)

_____   _____
(signature of witness)   (signature of witness)

_____   _____
(date)   (date)

Declaration Of A Desire For A Natural Death

I, _____, being of sound mind, desire that, as specified below, my life not be prolonged by extraordinary means or be artificial nutrition or hydration if my condition is determined to be terminal and incurable or if I am diagnosed as being in a persistent vegetative state. I am aware and understand that this writing authorizes a physician to withhold or discontinue extraordinary means or artificial nutrition or hydration, in accordance with my specifications set forth below:

(Initial any of the following, as desired):

_____ If my condition is determined to be terminal and incurable, I authorize the following:

                 _____ My physician may withhold or discontinue extraordinary means only.

                 _____ In addition to withholding or discontinuing extraordinary means if such means are necessary, my physician may withhold or discontinue either artificial nutrition or hydration, or both.

_____ If my physician determines that I am in a persistent vegetative state, I authorize the following:

                 _____ My physician may withhold or discontinue extraordinary means only.

                 _____ In addition to withholding or discontinuing extraordinary means if such means are necessary, my physician may withhold or discontinue either artificial nutrition or hydration, or both.

This the _____ day of _____, _____.

                               Signature _____

I hereby state that the declarant, _____, being of sound mind signed the above declaration in my presence and that I am not related to the declarant by blood or marriage and that I do not know or have a reasonable expectation that I would be entitled to any portion of the estate of the declarant under any existing will or codicil of the declarant or as an heir under the Intestate Succession Act if the declarant died on this date without a will. I also state that I am not the declarant's attending physician or an employee of the declarant's attending physician, or an employee of a health facility in which the declarant is a patient or an employee of a nursing home or any group-care home where the declarant resides. I further state that I do not now have any claim against the declarant.

                               Witness _____

                               Witness _____

The clerk or assistant clerk, of a notary public may, upon proper proof, certify the declaration as follows:

Certificate

I, _____, Clerk (Assistant Clerk) of Superior Court or Notary Public (circle one as appropriate) for _____ County hereby certify that _____, the declarant, appeared before me and swore to me and to the witnesses in my presence that this instrument is his Declaration Of A Desire For A Natural Death, and that he had willingly and voluntarily made and executed it as his free act and deed for the purposes expressed in it.

I further certify that _____ and _____, witnesses, appeared before me and swore that they witnessed _____, declarant, sign the attached declaration, believing him to be of sound mind; and also swore that at the time they witnessed the declaration (i) they were not related within the third degree to the declarant or to the declarant's spouse, and (ii) they did not know or have a reasonable expectation that they would be entitled to any portion of the estate of the declarant under any existing will of the declarant or codicil thereto then existing or under the Intestate Succession Act as it provided at that time, and (iii) they were not a physician attending the declarant or an employee of an attending physician or an employee of a health facility in which the declarant was a patient or an employee of a nursing home or any group-care home in which the declarant resided, and (iv) they did not have a claim against the declarant. I further certify that I am satisfied as to the genuineness and due execution of the declaration.

This the _____ day of _____, _____.

_____
Clerk (Assistant Clerk) of Superior Court or Notary Public (circle one as appropriate) for the County of _____

Declaration

I declare on _____ (month, day, year);

a.   I have made the following decision concerning life-prolonging treatment (initial 1, 2, or 3):

    (1)   _____   I direct that life-prolonging treatment be withheld or withdrawn and that I be permitted to die naturally if two physicians certify that:

        (a)   I am in a terminal condition that is an incurable or irreversible condition which, without the administration of life-prolonging treatment, will result in my imminent death;

        (b)   The application of life-prolonging treatment would serve only to artificially prolong the process of dying; and

        (c)   I am not pregnant.

    It is my intention that this declaration be honored by my family and physicians as the final expressions of my legal right to refuse medical and surgical treatment and that they accept the consequences of that refusal, which is death.

    (2)   _____   I direct that life-prolonging treatment, which could extend my life, be used if two physicians certify that I am in a terminal condition that is an incurable and irreversible condition which, without the administration of life-prolonging treatment, will result in my imminent death. It is my intention that this declaration be honored by my family and physicians as the final expressions of my legal right to direct that medical or surgical treatment be provided.

    (3)   _____   I make no statement concerning life-prolonging treatment.

b.   I have made the following decision concerning the administration of nutrition when my death is imminent (initial only one statement):

    (1)   _____   I wish to receive nutrition.

    (2)   _____   I wish to receive nutrition unless I cannot physically assimilate nutrition, nutrition would be physically harmful or would cause unreasonable physical pain, or nutrition would only prolong the process of my dying.

    (3)   _____   I do not wish to receive nutrition.

    (4)   _____   I make no statement concerning the administration of nutrition.

c.   I have made the following decision concerning the administration of hydration when my death is imminent (initial only one statement):

(1)   _____   I wish to receive hydration.

(2)   _____   I wish to receive hydration unless I cannot physically assimilate hydration, hydration would be physically harmful or would cause unreasonable physical pain, or hydration would only prolong the process of my dying.

(3)   _____   I do not wish to receive hydration.

(4)   _____   I make no statement concerning the administration of hydration.

d.   Concerning the administration of nutrition and hydration, I understand that if I make no statement about nutrition or hydration, my attending physician may withhold or withdraw nutrition or hydration if the physician determines that I cannot physically assimilate nutrition or hydration or that nutrition or hydration would be physically harmful or would cause unreasonable physical pain.

e.   If I have been diagnosed as pregnant and that diagnosis is known to my physician, this declaration is not effective during the course of my pregnancy.

f.   I understand the importance of this declaration, I am voluntarily signing this declaration, I am at least eighteen years of age, and I am emotionally and mentally competent to make this declaration.

g.   I understand that I may revoke this declaration at any time.

Signed _____

City, County, and State of Residence _____

The declarant is known to me and I believe the declarant to be of sound mind. I am not related to the declarant by blood or marriage, nor would I be entitled to any portion of the declarant's estate upon the declarant's death. I am not the declarant's attending physician, a person who has a claim against any portion of the declarant's estate upon the declarant's death, or a person directly financially responsible for the declarant's medical care.

Witness _____

Witness _____

DECLARATION

I, _____, being of sound mind, willfully and voluntarily make known my desires regarding my medical care and treatment under the circumstances as indicated below:

_____ 1. If I should be in a terminal condition as defined below, and if I am unable to make decisions regarding my medical treatment, I direct my attending physician to withhold or withdraw life-sustaining treatment and procedures that merely prolong the dying process and are not necessary to my comfort or to alleviate pain. This authorization includes, but is not limited to, the withholding or withdrawal of the following types of medical treatment (subject to any special instructions in paragraph 5 below):

        _____ a. Cardiopulmonary resuscitation (CPR) (this includes, but is not limited to, the use of drugs, electric shock, and artificial breathing).
        _____ b. Kidney dialysis.
        _____ c. Surgery or other invasive procedures.
        _____ d. Transfusions of blood or blood products.
        _____ e. Drugs and antibiotics.
        _____ f. Artificial nutrition and hydration.
        _____ g. Other: _____
_____

AS USED IN THIS DOCUMENT, THE TERM "TERMINAL CONDITION" MEANS AN IRREVERSIBLE, INCURABLE, AND UNTREATABLE CONDITION CAUSED BY DISEASE, ILLNESS, OR INJURY FROM WHICH, TO A REASONABLE DEGREE OF MEDICAL CERTAINTY AS DETERMINED IN ACCORDANCE WITH REASON-ABLE MEDICAL STANDARDS BY THE DECLARANT'S ATTENDING PHYSICIAN AND ONE OTHER PHYSICIAN WHO HAS EXAMINED THE DECLARANT, BOTH OF THE FOLLOWING APPLY:
(1) THERE CAN BE NO RECOVERY.
(2) DEATH IS LIKELY TO OCCUR WITHIN A RELATIVELY SHORT TIME IF LIFE-SUSTAINING TREATMENT IS NOT ADMINISTERED.

_____ 2. If I should be in a permanently unconscious state as defined below, I direct my attending physicians to withhold or withdraw life-sustaining treatment and procedures other than such medical treatment and procedures necessary to my comfort or to alleviate pain. This authorization includes, but is not limited to, the withholding or withdrawal of the following types of medical treatment (subject to any special instructions in paragraph 5 below):

        _____ a. Cardiopulmonary resuscitation (CPR) (this includes, but is not limited to, the use of drugs, electric shock, and artificial breathing).
        _____ b. Kidney dialysis.
        _____ c. Surgery or other invasive procedures.
        _____ d. Transfusions of blood or blood products.
        _____ e. Drugs and antibiotics.
        _____ g. Other: _____
_____
        _____ f. Artificial nutrition and hydration. MY ATTENDING PHYSICIAN IS AUTHORIZED TO WITHHOLD OR WITHDRAW NUTRITION AND HYDRATION IF I AM IN A PERMANENTLY UNCONSCIOUS STATE AND IF MY ATTENDING PHYSICIAN AND AT LEAST ONE OTHER PHYSICIAN WHO HAS EXAMINED ME DETERMINE, TO A REASONABLE DEGREE OF MEDICAL CERTAINTY AND IN ACCORDANCE WITH REASONABLE MEDICAL STANDARDS,

THAT NUTRITION OR HYDRATION WILL NOT OR NO LONGER WILL SERVE TO PROVIDE COMFORT TO ME OR ALLEVIATE MY PAIN.

_____
Signature of Declarant

_____ g. Other: _____

_____

AS USED IN THIS DOCUMENT, THE TERM "PERMANENTLY UNCONSCIOUS STATE" MEANS A STATE OF PERMANENT UNCONSCIOUSNESS IN THE DECLARANT THAT, TO A REASONABLE DEGREE OF MEDICAL CERTAINTY AS DETERMINED IN ACCORDANCE WITH REASONABLE MEDICAL STANDARDS BY THE DECLARANT'S ATTENDING PHYSICIAN AND ONE OTHER PHYSICIAN WHO HAS EXAMINED THE DECLARANT, IS CHARACTERIZED BY BOTH OF THE FOLLOWING:
(1) IRREVERSIBLE UNAWARENESS OF ONE'S BEING AND ENVIRONMENT.
(2) TOTAL LOSS OF CEREBRAL CORTICAL FUNCTIONING; RESULTING IN THE DECLARANT HAVING NO CAPACITY TO EXPERIENCE PAIN OR SUFFERING.

_____ 3. It is my desire that my attending physician notify the following persons, if available, in the event life-sustaining treatment is to be withheld or withdrawn pursuant to this declaration:

_____
_____
_____
_____

_____ 4. I want my life prolonged to the greatest extent possible (subject to any special instructions in paragraph 5 below).

_____ 5. Special instructions (if any) _____

_____
_____
_____

Signed this _____ day of _____,200____.

_____
Signature of declarant

Address:_____

_____

Witnesses

The declarant voluntarily signed this document in my presence, and appeared to be of sound mind and not under or subject to duress, fraud, or undue influence. I am an adult; am not related to the declarant by blood, marriage, or adoption; am not the attending physician of the declarant; and am not the administrator of any nursing home in which the declarant is receiving care.

Witness:_____   Witness_____

Name:_____   Name:_____

Address:_____   Address:_____

_____   _____

State of _____)

County of _____)

On this _____ day of _____, 200_____, before me, personally appeared _____, the declarant, who is personally known to me or who provided _____ as identification, who signed the foregoing instrument in my presence, and who appeared to be of sound mind and not under or subject to duress, fraud, or undue influence.

_____

Notary Public

Advance Directive for Health Care

I, _____, being of sound mind and eighteen (18) years of age or older, willfully and voluntarily make known my desire, by my instructions to others through my living will, or by my appointment of a health care proxy, or both, that my life shall not be artificially prolonged under the circumstances set forth below. I thus do hereby declare:

I. Living Will

a. If my attending physician and another physician determine that I am no longer able to make decisions regarding my medical treatment, I direct my attending physician and other health care providers, pursuant to the Oklahoma Rights of the Terminally Ill or Persistently Unconscious Act, to withhold or withdraw treatment from me under the circumstances I have indicated below by my signature. I understand that I will be given treatment that is necessary for my comfort or to alleviate my pain.

b. If I have a terminal condition:

(1) I direct that life-sustaining treatment shall be withheld or withdrawn if such treatment would only prolong my process of dying, and if my attending physician and another physician determine that I have an incurable and irreversible condition that even with the administration of life-sustaining treatment will cause my death within six (6) months.
_____ (initials)

(2) I understand that the subject of the artificial administration of nutrition and hydration (food and water) that will only prolong the process of dying from an incurable and irreversible condition is of particular importance. I understand that if I do not sign this paragraph, artificially administered nutrition and hydration will be administered to me. I further understand that if I sign this paragraph, I am authorizing the withholding or withdrawal of artificially administered nutrition (food) and hydration (water).
_____ (initials)

(3) I direct that (add other medical directives, if any) _____

_____

_____

_____(initials)

c. If I am persistently unconscious:

(1) I direct that life-sustaining treatment be withheld or withdrawn if such treatment will only serve to maintain me in an irreversible condition, as determined by my attending physician and another physician, in which thought and awareness of self and environment are absent. _____ (initials)

(2) I understand that the subject of the artificial administration of nutrition and hydration (food and water) for individuals who have become persistently unconscious is of particular importance. I understand that if I do not sign this paragraph, artificially administered nutrition and hydration will be administered to me. I further understand that if I sign this paragraph, I am authorizing the withholding or withdrawal of artificially administered nutrition (food) and hydration (water). _____ (initials)

(3) I direct that (add other medical directives, if any) _____
_____
_____
_____
_____(initials)

II. My Appointment of My Health Care Proxy

a. If my attending physician and another physician determine that I am no longer able to make decisions regarding my medical treatment, I direct my attending physician and other health care providers pursuant to the Oklahoma Rights of the Terminally Ill or Persistently Unconscious Act to follow the instructions of _____, whom I appoint as my health care proxy. If my health care proxy is unable or unwilling to serve, I appoint _____ as my alternate health care proxy with the same authority. My health care proxy is authorized to make whatever medical treatment decisions I could make if I were able, except that decisions regarding life-sustaining treatment can be made by my health care proxy or alternate health care proxy only as I indicate in the following sections.

b. If I have a terminal condition:

(1) I authorize my health care proxy to direct that life-sustaining treatment be withheld or withdrawn if such treatment would only prolong my process of dying and if my attending physician and another physician determine that I have an incurable and irreversible condition that even with the administration of life-sustaining treatment will cause my death within six (6) months. _____ (initials)

(2) I understand that the subject of the artificial administration of nutrition and hydration (food and water) is of particular importance. I understand that if I do not sign this paragraph, artificially administered nutrition (food) or hydration (water) will be administered to me. I further understand that if I sign this paragraph, I am authorizing the withholding or withdrawal of artificially administered nutrition and hydration.

_____ (initials)

(3) I authorize my health care proxy to (add other medical directives, if any) _____
_____
_____
_____

_____ (initials)

c. If I am persistently unconscious:

(1) I authorize my health care proxy to direct that life-sustaining treatment be withheld or withdrawn if such treatment will only serve to maintain me in an irreversible condition, as determined by my attending physician and another physician, in which thought and awareness of self and environment are absent.

_____ (initials)

(2) I understand that the subject of the artificial administration of nutrition and hydration (food and water) is of particular importance. I understand that if I do not sign this paragraph, artificially administered nutrition (food) and hydration (water) will be administered to me. I further understand that if I sign this paragraph, I am authorizing the withholding and withdrawal of artificially administered nutrition and hydration.

_____ (initials)

(3) I authorize my health care proxy to (add other medical directives, if any) _____
_____
_____

_____ (initials)

III. Anatomical Gifts

I direct that at the time of my death my entire body or designated body organs or body parts be donated for purposes of transplantation, therapy, advancement of medical or dental science or research or education pursuant to the provisions of the Uniform Anatomical Gift Act. Death means either irreversible cessation of circulatory and respiratory functions or irreversible cessation of all functions of the entire brain, including the brain stem. I specifically donate:

☐ My entire body; or

☐ The following body organs or parts:

( ) lungs,   ( ) liver,   ( ) pancreas,   ( ) heart,   ( ) kidneys,

( ) brain,   ( ) skin,   ( ) bones/marrow,   ( ) bloods/fluids, ( ) tissue,

( ) arteries,   ( ) eyes/cornea/lens,   ( ) glands, ( ) other _____

_____ (initials)

IV. Conflicting Provision

I understand that if I have completed both a living will and have appointed a health care proxy, and if there is a conflict between my health care proxy's decision and my living will, my living will shall take precedence unless I indicate otherwise. _____

_____
_____ (initials)

V. General Provisions

a. I understand that if I have been diagnosed as pregnant and that diagnosis is known to my attending physician, this advance directive shall have no force or effect during the course of my pregnancy.

b. In the absence of my ability to give directions regarding the use of life-sustaining procedures, it is my intention that this advance directive shall be honored by my family and physicians as the final expression of my legal right to refuse medical or surgical treatment including, but not limited to, the administration of any life-sustaining procedures, and I accept the consequences of such refusal.

c. This advance directive shall be in effect until it is revoked.

d. I understand that I may revoke this advance directive at any time.

e. I understand and agree that if I have any prior directives, and if I sign this advance directive, my prior directives are revoked.

f. I understand the full importance of this advance directive and I am emotionally and mentally competent to make this advance directive.

Signed this _____ day of _____, 20 _____.

_____
(Signature)

_____
City, County and State of Residence

This advance directive was signed in my presence.

_____   _____
(Signature of Witness)   (Signature of Witness)

_____   _____
_____   _____
(Address)   (Address)

ADVANCE DIRECTIVE

<u>YOU DO NOT HAVE TO FILL OUT AND SIGN THIS FORM</u>

<u>PART A: IMPORTANT INFORMATION ABOUT THIS ADVANCE DIRECTIVE</u>

This is an important legal document. It can control critical decisions about your health care. Before signing, consider these important facts:

<u>Facts About Part B</u>

<u>(Appointing a Health Care Representative)</u>

You have the right to name a person to direct your health care when you cannot do so. This person is called your "health care representative." You can do this by using Part B of this form. Your representative must accept on Part E of this form.

You can write in this document any restrictions you want on how your representative will make decisions for you. Your representative must follow your desires as stated in this document or otherwise made known. If your desires are unknown, your representative must try to act in your best interest. Your representative can resign at any time.

<u>Facts About Part C</u>

<u>(Giving Health Care Instructions)</u>

You also have the right to give instructions for health care providers to follow if you become unable to direct your care. You can do this by using Part C of this form.

<u>Facts About Completing This Form</u>

This form is valid only if you sign it voluntarily and when you are of sound mind. If you do not want an advance directive, you do not have to sign this form.

Unless you have limited the duration of this advance directive, it will not expire. If you have set an expiration date, and you become unable to direct your health care before that date, this advance directive will not expire until you are able to make those decisions again.

You may revoke this document at any time. To do so, notify your representative and your health care provider of the revocation.

Despite this document, you have the right to decide your own health care as long as you are able to do so.

If there is anything in this document that you do not understand, ask a lawyer to explain it to you.

You may sign PART B, PART C, or both parts. You may cross out words that don't express your wishes or add words that better express your wishes. Witnesses must sign PART D.

Print your NAME, BIRTHDATE AND ADDRESS here:

_____   _____

(Name)   (Birthdate)

_____

_____

(Address)

Unless revoked or suspended, this advance directive will continue for:

INITIAL ONE:

_____ My entire life

_____ Other period (_____ Years)

PART B: APPOINTMENT OF HEALTH CARE REPRESENTATIVE

I appoint _____ as my health care representative. My representative's address is _____ and telephone number is _____.

I appoint _____ as my alternate health care representative. My alternate's address is _____ and telephone number is _____.

I authorize my representative (or alternate) to direct my health care when I can't do so.

NOTE: You may not appoint your doctor, an employee of your doctor, or an owner, operator or employee of your health care facility, unless that person is related to you by blood, marriage or adoption or that person was appointed before your admission into the health care facility.

1. Limits.
Special Conditions or Instructions:

_____

_____

_____

INITIAL IF THIS APPLIES:

_____ I have executed a Health Care Instruction or Directive to Physicians. My representative is to honor it.

2. Life Support.

"Life support" refers to any medical means for maintaining life, including procedures, devices and medications. If you refuse life support, you will still get routine measures to keep you clean and comfortable.

INITIAL IF THIS APPLIES:

_____ My representative MAY decide about life support for me. (If you don't initial this space, then your representative MAY NOT decide about life support.)

3. Tube Feeding.

One sort of life support is food and water supplied artificially by medical device, known as tube feeding.

INITIAL IF THIS APPLIES:

_____ My representative MAY decide about tube feeding for me. (If you don't initial this space, then your representative MAY NOT decide about tube feeding.)

_____
(Date)

SIGN HERE TO APPOINT A HEALTH CARE REPRESENTATIVE

_____
(Signature of person making appointment)

PART C: HEALTH CARE INSTRUCTIONS

NOTE: In filling out these instructions, keep the following in mind:

• The term "as my physician recommends" means that you want your physician to try life support if your physician believes it could be helpful and then discontinue it if it is not helping your health condition or symptoms.

• "Life support" and "tube feeding" are defined in Part B above.

• If you refuse tube feeding, you should understand that malnutrition, dehydration and death will probably result.

• You will get care for your comfort and cleanliness, no matter what choices you make.

• You may either give specific instructions by filling out Items 1 to 4 below, or you may use the general instruction provided by Item 5.

• Here are my desires about my health care if my doctor and another knowledgeable doctor confirm that I am in a medical condition described below:

1. <u>Close to Death.</u> If I am close to death and life support would only postpone the moment of my death:

A. INITIAL ONE:

_____ I want to receive tube feeding.

_____ I want tube feeding only as my physician recommends.

_____ I DO NOT WANT tube feeding.

B. INITIAL ONE:

_____ I want any other life support that may apply.

_____ I want life support only as my physician recommends.

_____ I want NO life support.

2. <u>Permanently Unconscious.</u> If I am unconscious and it is very unlikely that I will ever become conscious again:

A. INITIAL ONE:

_____ I want to receive tube feeding.

_____ I want tube feeding only as my physician recommends.

_____ I DO NOT WANT tube feeding.

B. INITIAL ONE:

_____ I want any other life support that may apply.

_____ I want life support only as my physician recommends.

_____ I want NO life support.

3. <u>Advanced Progressive Illness.</u> If I have a progressive illness that will be fatal and is in an advanced stage, and I am consistently and permanently unable to communicate by any means, swallow food and water safely, care for myself and recognize my family and other people, and it is very unlikely that my condition will substantially improve:

A. INITIAL ONE:

_____ I want to receive tube feeding.

_____ I want tube feeding only as my physician recommends.

_____ I DO NOT WANT tube feeding.

B. INITIAL ONE:

_____ I want any other life support that may apply.

_____ I want life support only as my physician recommends.

_____ I want NO life support.

4. <u>Extraordinary Suffering.</u> If life support would not help my medical condition and would make me suffer permanent and severe pain:

A. INITIAL ONE:

_____ I want to receive tube feeding.

_____ I want tube feeding only as my physician recommends.

_____ I DO NOT WANT tube feeding.

B. INITIAL ONE:

_____ I want any other life support that may apply.

_____ I want life support only as my physician recommends.

_____ I want NO life support.

5. <u>General Instruction.</u>

INITIAL IF THIS APPLIES:

_____ I do not want my life to be prolonged by life support. I also do not want tube feeding as life support. I want my doctors to allow me to die naturally if my doctor and another knowledgeable doctor confirm I am in any of the medical conditions listed in Items 1 to 4 above.

6. <u>Additional Conditions or Instructions.</u>

_____

_____

_____

(Insert description of what you want done.)

7. <u>Other Documents.</u> A "health care power of attorney" is any document you may have signed to appoint a representative to make health care decisions for you.

INITIAL ONE:

_____ I have previously signed a health care power of attorney. I want it to remain in effect unless I appointed a health care representative after signing the health care power of attorney.

_____ I have a health care power of attorney, and I REVOKE IT.

_____ I DO NOT have a health care power of attorney.

_____
(Date)

SIGN HERE TO GIVE INSTRUCTIONS

_____
(Signature)

PART D: DECLARATION OF WITNESSES

We declare that the person signing this advance directive:

(a) Is personally known to us or has provided proof of identity;

(b) Signed or acknowledged that person's signature on this advance directive in our presence;

(c) Appears to be of sound mind and not under duress, fraud or undue influence;

(d) Has not appointed either of us as health care representative or alternative representative; and

(e) Is not a patient for whom either of us is attending physician.

Witnessed By:

_____   _____
(Signature of Witness)   (Printed Name of Witness)

_____   _____
(Signature of Witness)   (Printed Name of Witness)

NOTE: One witness must not be a relative (by blood, marriage or adoption) of the person signing this advance directive. That witness must also not be entitled to any portion of the person's estate upon death. That witness must also not own, operate or be employed at a health care facility where the person is a patient or resident.

PART E: ACCEPTANCE BY HEALTH CARE REPRESENTATIVE

I accept this appointment and agree to serve as health care representative. I understand I must act consistently with the desires of the person I represent, as expressed in this advance directive or otherwise made known to me. If I do not know the desires of the person I represent, I have a duty to act in what I believe in good faith to be that person's best interest. I understand that this document allows me to decide about that person's health care only while that person cannot do so. I understand that the person who appointed me may revoke this appointment. If I learn that this document has been suspended or revoked, I will inform the person's current health care provider if known to me.

_____

(Signature of Health Care Representative/Date)

_____

(Printed name)

_____

(Signature of Alternate Health Care Representative/Date)

_____

(Printed name)

DECLARATION

I, _____, being of sound mind, willfully and voluntarily make this declaration to be followed if I become incompetent. This declaration reflects my firm and settled commitment to refuse life-sustaining treatment under the circumstances indicated below.

I direct my attending physician to withhold or withdraw life-sustaining treatment that serves only to prolong the process of my dying, if I should be in a terminal condition or in a state of permanent unconsciousness.

I direct that treatment be limited to measures to keep me comfortable and to relieve pain, including any pain that might occur by withholding or withdrawing life-sustaining treatment.

In addition, if I am in the condition described above, I feel especially strong about the following forms of treatment:

I ( ) do ( ) do not want cardiac resuscitation.

I ( ) do ( ) do not want mechanical respiration.

I ( ) do ( ) do not want tube feeding or any other artificial or invasive form of nutrition (food) or hydration (water).

I ( ) do ( ) do not want blood or blood products.

I ( ) do ( ) do not want any form of surgery or invasive diagnostic tests.

I ( ) do ( ) do not want kidney dialysis.

I ( ) do ( ) do not want antibiotics.

I realize that if I do not specifically indicate my preference regarding any of the forms of treatment listed above, I may receive that form of treatment.

Other instructions:

I ( ) do ( ) do not want to designate another person as my surrogate to make medical treatment decisions for me if I should be incompetent and in a terminal condition or in a state of permanent unconsciousness. Name and address of surrogate (if applicable):

Name and address of substitute surrogate (if surrogate above is unable to serve):

I ( ) do ( ) do not want to make an anatomical gift of all or part of my body, subject to the following limitations, if any:

I made this declaration on the _____ day of _____ (month) (year).

_____
Declarant's signature

_____
Declarant's address

The declarant or the person on behalf of and at the direction of declarant knowingly and voluntarily signed this writing by signature or mark in my presence.

_____
Witness' signature

_____
Witness' signature

_____
Witness' address

_____
Witness' address

DECLARATION

I, _____, being of sound mind willfully and voluntarily make known my desire that my dying shall not be artificially prolonged under the circumstances set forth below, do hereby declare:

If I should have an incurable or irreversible condition that will cause my death within a relatively short time, and if I am unable to make decisions regarding my medical treatment, I direct my attending physician to withhold or withdraw procedures that merely prolong the dying process and are not necessary to my comfort, or to alleviate pain.

This authorization includes ( ) does not include ( ) the withholding or withdrawal of artificial feeding (check only one box above).

Signed this _____ day of _____, 200_____.

_____
Signature

_____
_____
Address

The declarant is personally known to me and voluntarily signed this document in my presence.

_____   _____
Witness   Witness

_____   _____

STATUTORY FORM
DURABLE POWER OF ATTORNEY FOR HEALTH CARE

WARNING TO PERSON EXECUTING THIS DOCUMENT

This is an important legal document which is authorized by the general laws of this state. Before executing this document, you should know these important facts:

You must be at least eighteen (18) years of age and a resident of the state for this document to be legally valid and binding.

This document gives the person you designate as your agent (the attorney in fact) the power to make health care decisions for you. Your agent must act consistently with your desires as stated in this document or otherwise made known.

Except as you otherwise specify in this document, this document gives your agent the power to consent to your doctor not giving treatment or stopping treatment necessary to keep you alive.

Notwithstanding this document, you have the right to make medical and other health care decisions for yourself so long as you can give informed consent with respect to the particular decision. In addition, no treatment may be given to you over your objection at the time, and health care necessary to keep you alive may not be stopped or withheld if you object at the time.

This document gives your agent authority to consent, to refuse to consent, or to withdraw consent to any care, treatment, service, or procedure to maintain, diagnose, or treat a physical or mental condition. This power is subject to any statement of your desires and any limitation that you include in this document. You may state in this document any types of treatment that you do not desire. In addition, a court can take away the power of your agent to make health care decisions for you if your agent:

(1) Authorizes anything that is illegal,

(2) Acts contrary to your known desires, or

(3) Where your desires are not known, does anything that is clearly contrary to your best interests.

Unless you specify a specific period, this power will exist until you revoke it. Your agent's power and authority ceases upon your death except to inform your family or next of kin of your desire, if any, to be an organ and tissue owner.

You have the right to revoke the authority of your agent by notifying your agent or your treating doctor, hospital, or other health care provider orally or in writing of the revocation.

Your agent has the right to examine your medical records and to consent to their disclosure unless you limit this right in this document.

This document revokes any prior durable power of attorney for health care.

You should carefully read and follow the witnessing procedure described at the end of this form. This document will not be valid unless you comply with the witnessing procedure.

If there is anything in this document that you do not understand, you should ask a lawyer to explain it to you.

Your agent may need this document immediately in case of an emergency that requires a decision concerning your health care. Either keep this document where it is immediately available to your agent and alternate agents or give each of them an executed copy of this document. You may also want to give your doctor an executed copy of this document.

(1) DESIGNATION OF HEALTH CARE AGENT.

I,_____

_____

(insert your name and address)

do hereby designate and appoint

_____

_____

(insert name, address, and telephone number of one individual only as your agent to make health care decisions for you. None of the following may be designated as your agent: (1) your treating health care provider, (2) a nonrelative employee of your treating health care provider, (3) an operator of a community care facility, or (4) a nonrelative employee of an operator of a community care facility.) as my attorney in fact (agent) to make health care decisions for me as authorized in this document. For the purposes of this document, "health care decision" means consent, refusal of consent, or withdrawal of consent to any care, treatment, service, or procedure to maintain, diagnose, or treat an individual's physical or mental condition.

(2) CREATION OF DURABLE POWER OF ATTORNEY FOR HEALTH CARE. By this document I intend to create a durable power of attorney for health care.

(3) GENERAL STATEMENT OF AUTHORITY GRANTED. Subject to any limitations in this document, I hereby grant to my agent full power and authority to make health care decisions for me to the same extent that I could make such decisions for myself if I had the capacity to do so. In exercising this authority, my agent shall make health care decisions that are consistent with my desires as stated in this document or otherwise made known to my agent, including, but not limited to, my desires concerning obtaining or refusing or withdrawing life-prolonging care, treatment, services, and procedures and informing my family or next of kin of my desire, if any, to be an organ or tissue donor.

(If you want to limit the authority of your agent to make health care decisions for you, you can state the limitations in paragraph (4) ("Statement of Desires, Special Provisions, and Limitations") below. You can indicate your desires by including a statement of your desires in the same paragraph.)

(4) STATEMENT OF DESIRES, SPECIAL PROVISIONS, AND LIMITATIONS. (Your agent must make health care decisions that are consistent with your known desires. You can, but are not required to, state your desires in the space provided below. You should consider whether you want to include a statement of your desires concerning life-prolonging care, treatment, services, and procedures. You can also include a statement of your desires concerning other matters relating to your health care. You can also make your desires known to your agent by discussing your desires with your agent or by some other means. If there are any types of treatment that you do not want to be used, you should state them in the space below. If you want to limit in any other way the authority given your agent by this document, you should state the limits in the space below. If you do not state any limits, your agent will have broad powers to make health care decisions for you, except to the extent that there are limits provided by law.)

In exercising the authority under this durable power of attorney for health care, my agent shall act consistently with my desires as stated below and is subject to the special provisions and limitations stated below:

(a) Statement of desires concerning life-prolonging care, treatment, services, and procedures:

(b) Additional statement of desires, special provisions, and limitations regarding health care decisions:

(c) Statement of desire regarding organ and tissue donation:

Initial if applicable:

[   ] In the event of my death, I request that my agent inform my family/next of kin of my desire to be an organ and tissue donor, if possible.

(You may attach additional pages if you need more space to complete your statement. If you attach additional pages, you must date and sign EACH of the additional pages at the same time you date and sign this document.)

(5) INSPECTION AND DISCLOSURE OF INFORMATION RELATING TO MY PHYSICAL OR MENTAL HEALTH. Subject to any limitations in this document, my agent has the power and authority to do all of the following:

(a) Request, review, and receive any information, verbal or written, regarding my physical or mental health, including, but not limited to, medical and hospital records.

(b) Execute on my behalf any releases or other documents that may be required in order to obtain this information.

(c) Consent to the disclosure of this information.

(If you want to limit the authority of your agent to receive and disclose information relating to your health, you must state the limitations in paragraph (4) ("Statement of desires, special provisions, and limitations") above.)

(6) SIGNING DOCUMENTS, WAIVERS, AND RELEASES. Where necessary to implement the health care decisions that my agent is authorized by this document to make, my agent has the power and authority to execute on my behalf all of the following:

(a) Documents titled or purporting to be a "Refusal to Permit Treatment" and "Leaving Hospital Against Medical Advice."

(b) Any necessary waiver or release from liability required by a hospital or physician.

(7) DURATION. (Unless you specify a shorter period in the space below, this power of attorney will exist until it is revoked.)

This durable power of attorney for health care expires on _____

(Fill in this space ONLY if you want the authority of your agent to end on a specific date.)

(8) DESIGNATION OF ALTERNATE AGENTS. (You are not required to designate any alternate agents but you may do so. Any alternate agent you designate will be able to make the same health care decisions as the agent you designated in paragraph (1), above, in the event that agent is unable

or ineligible to act as your agent. If the agent you designated is your spouse, he or she becomes ineligible to act as your agent if your marriage is dissolved.)

If the person designated as my agent in paragraph (1) is not available or becomes ineligible to act as my agent to make a health care decision for me or loses the mental capacity to make health care decisions for me, or if I revoke that person's appointment or authority to act as my agent to make health care decisions for me, then I designate and appoint the following persons to serve as my agent to make health care decisions for me as authorized in this document, such persons to serve in the order listed below:

(A) First Alternate Agent: _____

_____
(Insert name, address, and telephone number of first alternate agent.)

(B) Second Alternate Agent: _____

_____
(Insert name, address, and telephone number of second alternate agent.)

(9) PRIOR DESIGNATIONS REVOKED. I revoke any prior durable power of attorney for health care.

DATE AND SIGNATURE OF PRINCIPAL

(YOU MUST DATE AND SIGN THIS POWER OF ATTORNEY)

I sign my name to this Statutory Form Durable Power of Attorney for Health Care on

_____ at _____, _____.
(Date)   (City)   (State)

_____
(You sign here)

(THIS POWER OF ATTORNEY WILL NOT BE VALID UNLESS IT IS SIGNED BY TWO (2) QUALIFIED WITNESSES WHO ARE PRESENT WHEN YOU SIGN OR ACKNOWLEDGE YOUR SIGNATURE. IF YOU HAVE ATTACHED ANY ADDITIONAL PAGES TO THIS FORM, YOU MUST DATE AND SIGN EACH OF THE ADDITIONAL PAGES AT THE SAME TIME YOU DATE AND SIGN THIS POWER OF ATTORNEY.) YOU ARE NOT REQUIRED TO HAVE THIS POWER OF ATTORNEY NOTARIZED.

STATEMENT OF WITNESSES

(This document must be witnessed by two (2) qualified adult witnesses or one (1) notary public. None of the following may be used as a witness:

(1) A person you designate as your agent or alternate agent,

(2) A health care provider,

(3) An employee of a health care provider,

(4) The operator of a community care facility,

(5) An employee of an operator of a community care facility.

You are not required to have this document witnessed by a notary public.

At least one of the qualified witnesses or the notary public must make the additional declaration set out following the place where the witnesses sign.)

I declare under penalty of perjury that the person who signed or acknowledged this document is personally known to me to be the principal, that the principal signed or acknowledged this durable power of attorney in my presence, that the principal appears to be of sound mind and under no duress, fraud, or undue influence, that I am not the person appointed as attorney in fact by this document, and that I am not a health care provider, an employee of a health care provider, the operator of a community care facility, nor an employee of an operator of a community care facility.

Signature: _____   Residence Address:_____

Print Name: _____   _____

Date: _____

Signature: _____   Residence Address:_____

Print Name: _____   _____

Date: _____

(AT LEAST ONE OF THE ABOVE WITNESSES MUST ALSO SIGN THE FOLLOWING DECLARATION.)

I further declare under penalty of perjury that I am not related to the principal by blood, marriage, or adoption, and, to the best of my knowledge, I am not entitled to any part of the estate of the principal upon the death of the principal under a will now existing or by operation of law.

Signature:_____   Signature: _____

Print Name: _____   Print Name: _____

STATE OF SOUTH CAROLINA
COUNTY OF_____

DECLARATION
OF A DESIRE FOR A
NATURAL DEATH

I,_____, Declarant, being at least eighteen years of age and a resident of and domiciled in the City of_____, County of_____, State of South Carolina, make this Declaration this ___ day of_____, 200_____.

I wilfully and voluntarily make known my desire that no life-sustaining procedures be used to prolong my dying if my condition is terminal or if I am in a state of permanent unconsciousness, and I declare:

If at any time I have a condition certified to be a terminal condition by two physicians who have personally examined me, one of whom is my attending physician, and the physicians have determined that my death could occur within a reasonably short period of time without the use of life-sustaining procedures or if the physicians certify that I am in a state of permanent unconsciousness and where the application of life-sustaining procedures would serve only to prolong the dying process, I direct that the procedures be withheld or withdrawn, and that I be permitted to die naturally with only the administration of medication or the performance of any medical procedure necessary to provide me with comfort care.

INSTRUCTIONS CONCERNING ARTIFICIAL NUTRITION AND HYDRATION

INITIAL ONE OF THE FOLLOWING STATEMENTS

If my condition is terminal and could result in death within a reasonably short time,

_____ I direct that nutrition and hydration BE PROVIDED through any medically indicated means, including medically or surgically implanted tubes.

_____ I direct that nutrition and hydration NOT BE PROVIDED through any medically indicated means, including medically or surgically implanted tubes.

INITIAL ONE OF THE FOLLOWING STATEMENTS

If I am in a persistent vegetative state or other condition of permanent unconsciousness,

_____ I direct that nutrition and hydration BE PROVIDED through any medically indicated means, including medically or surgically implanted tubes.

_____ I direct that nutrition and hydration NOT BE PROVIDED through any medically indicated means, including medically or surgically implanted tubes.

In the absence of my ability to give directions regarding the use of life-sustaining procedures, it is my intention that this Declaration be honored by my family and physicians and any health facility in which I may be a patient as the final expression of my legal right to refuse medical or surgical treatment, and I accept the consequences from the refusal.

I am aware that this Declaration authorizes a physician to withhold or withdraw life-sustaining procedures. I am emotionally and mentally competent to make this Declaration.

APPOINTMENT OF AN AGENT (OPTIONAL)

1. You may give another person authority to revoke this declaration on your behalf. If you wish to do so, please enter that person's name in the space below.
Name of Agent with Power to Revoke:_____
Address:_____
Telephone Number:_____

2. You may give another person authority to enforce this declaration on your behalf. If you wish to do so, please enter that person's name in the space below.
Name of Agent with Power to Enforce: _____
Address:_____
Telephone Number:_____

REVOCATION PROCEDURES

THIS DECLARATION MAY BE REVOKED BY ANY ONE OF THE FOLLOWING METHODS. HOWEVER, A REVOCATION IS NOT EFFECTIVE UNTIL IT IS COMMUNICATED TO THE ATTENDING PHYSICIAN.

(1) BY BEING DEFACED, TORN, OBLITERATED, OR OTHERWISE DESTROYED, IN EXPRESSION OF YOUR INTENT TO REVOKE, BY YOU OR BY SOME PERSON IN YOUR PRESENCE AND BY YOUR DIRECTION. REVOCATION BY DESTRUCTION OF ONE OR MORE OF MULTIPLE ORIGINAL DECLARATIONS REVOKES ALL OF THE ORIGINAL DECLARATIONS;

(2) BY A WRITTEN REVOCATION SIGNED AND DATED BY YOU EXPRESSING YOUR INTENT TO REVOKE;

(3) BY YOUR ORAL EXPRESSION OF YOUR INTENT TO REVOKE THE DECLARATION. AN ORAL REVOCATION COMMUNICATED TO THE ATTENDING PHYSICIAN BY A PERSON OTHER THAN YOU IS EFFECTIVE ONLY IF:

    (a) THE PERSON WAS PRESENT WHEN THE ORAL REVOCATION WAS MADE;

    (b) THE REVOCATION WAS COMMUNICATED TO THE PHYSICIAN WITHIN A REASONABLE TIME;

    (c) YOUR PHYSICAL OR MENTAL CONDITION MAKES IT IMPOSSIBLE FOR THE PHYSICIAN TO CONFIRM THROUGH SUBSEQUENT CONVERSATION WITH YOU THAT THE REVOCATION HAS OCCURRED.

TO BE EFFECTIVE AS A REVOCATION, THE ORAL EXPRESSION CLEARLY MUST INDICATE YOUR DESIRE THAT THE DECLARATION NOT BE GIVEN EFFECT OR THAT LIFE-SUSTAINING PROCEDURES BE ADMINISTERED;

(4) IF YOU, IN THE SPACE ABOVE, HAVE AUTHORIZED AN AGENT TO REVOKE THE DECLARATION, THE AGENT MAY REVOKE ORALLY OR BY A WRITTEN, SIGNED, AND DATED INSTRUMENT. AN AGENT MAY REVOKE ONLY IF YOU ARE INCOMPETENT TO DO SO. AN AGENT MAY REVOKE THE DECLARATION PERMANENTLY OR TEMPORARILY.

(5) BY YOUR EXECUTING ANOTHER DECLARATION AT A LATER TIME.

_____
Signature of Declarant

STATE OF _____   AFFIDAVIT

COUNTY OF _____

We, _____ and _____, The undersigned witnesses to the foregoing Declaration, dated the _____ day of _____, 200_____, at least one of being first duly sworn, declare to the undersigned authority, on the basis of our best information and belief, that the Declaration was on that date signed by the declarant as and for his DECLARATION OF A DESIRE FOR A NATURAL DEATH in our presence and we, at his request and in his presence, and in the presence of each other subscribe our names as witnesses on that date. The declarant is personally known to us, and we believe him to be of sound mind. Each of us affirms that he is qualified as a witness to this Declaration under the provisions of the South Carolina Death With Dignity Act in that he is not related to the declarant by blood, marriage, or adoption, either as a spouse, lineal ancestor, descendant of the parents of the declarant, or spouse of any of them; nor directly financially responsible for the declarant's medical care; nor entitled to any portion of the declarant's estate upon his decease, whether under any will or as an heir by intestate succession, nor the beneficiary of a life insurance policy of the declarant; nor the declarant's attending physician; nor an employee of the attending physician; nor a person who has a claim against the declarant's decedent's estate as of this time. No more than one of us is an employee of a health facility in which the declarant is a patient. If the declarant is a resident in a hospital or nursing care facility at the date of execution of this Declaration, at least one of us is an ombudsman designated by the State Ombudsman, Office of the Governor.

_____   _____
Witness   Witness

    Subscribed before me by _____, the declarant, and subscribed and sworn to before me by_____, the witnesses, this _____ day of _____, 200_____.

_____
Signature

Notary Public for _____

My commission expires:_____

                                         SEAL

LIVING WILL DECLARATION

This is an important legal document. This document directs the medical treatment you are to receive in the event you are unable to participate in your own medical decisions and you are in a terminal condition. This document may state what kind of treatment you want or do not want to receive.

This document can control whether you live or die. Prepare this document carefully. If you use this form, read it completely. You may want to seek professional help to make sure the form does what you intend and is completed without mistakes.

This document will remain valid and in effect until and unless you revoke it. Review this document periodically to make sure it continues to reflect your wishes. You may amend or revoke this document at any time by notifying your physician and other health-care providers. You should give copies of this Document to your physician and your family. This form is entirely optional. If you choose to use this form, please note that the form provides signature lines for you, the two witnesses whom you have selected and a notary public.

TO MY FAMILY, PHYSICIANS, AND ALL THOSE CONCERNED WITH MY CARE:

I,_____ willfully and voluntarily make this declaration as a directive to be followed if I am in a terminal condition and become unable to participate in decisions regarding my medical care.

With respect to any life-sustaining treatment, I direct the following:

(Initial only one of the following optional directives if you agree. If you do not agree with any of the following directives, space is provided below for you to write your own directives).

_____ NO LIFE-SUSTAINING TREATMENT. I direct that no life-sustaining treatment be provided. If life-sustaining treatment is begun, terminate it.

_____ TREATMENT FOR RESTORATION. Provide life-sustaining treatment only if and for so long as you believe treatment offers a reasonable possibility of restoring to me the ability to think and act for myself.

_____ TREAT UNLESS PERMANENTLY UNCONSCIOUS. If you believe that I am permanently unconscious and are satisfied that this condition is irreversible, then do not provide me with life-sustaining treatment, and if life-sustaining treatment is being provided to me, terminate it. If and so long as you believe that treatment has a reasonable possibility of restoring consciousness to me, then provide life-sustaining treatment.

_____ MAXIMUM TREATMENT. Preserve my life as long as possible, but do not provide treatment that is not in accordance with accepted medical standards as then in effect.

(Artificial nutrition and hydration is food and water provided by means of a nasogastric tube or tubes inserted into the stomach, intestines, or veins. If you do not wish to receive this form of treatment, you must initial the statement below which reads: "I intend to include this treatment, among the 'life-sustaining treatment' that may be withheld or withdrawn.")

With respect to artificial nutrition and hydration, I wish to make clear that (Initial only one)

_____ I intend to include this treatment among the "life-sustaining treatment" that may be with-held or withdrawn.

_____ I do not intend to include this treatment among the "life-sustaining treatment" that may be withheld or withdrawn.

(If you do not agree with any of the printed directives and want to write your own, or if you want to write directives in addition to the printed provisions, or if you want to express some of your other thoughts, you can do so here.)

_____

_____

_____

Date:_____   _____

                                             (your signature)

_____   _____

(your address)   (type or print your signature)

The declarant voluntarily signed this document in my presence.

Witness _____   Witness_____

Address _____   Address _____

On this _____ day of_____, 200_____, the declarant, _____, and witnesses _____ , and _____, personally appeared before the undersigned officer and signed the foregoing instrument in my presence. Dated this _____ day of _____, 200____.

_____

Notary Public
My commission expires: _____

LIVING WILL

I, _____, willfully and voluntarily make known my desire that my dying shall not be artificially prolonged under the circumstances set forth below, and do hereby declare:

If at any time I should have a terminal condition and my attending physician has determined there is no reasonable medical expectation of recovery and which, as a medical probability, will result in my death, regardless of the use or discontinuance of medical treatment implemented for the purpose of sustaining life, or the life process, I direct that medical care be withheld or withdrawn, and that I be permitted to die naturally with only the administration of medications or the performance of any medical procedure deemed necessary to provide me with comfortable care or to alleviate pain.

ARTIFICIALLY PROVIDED NOURISHMENT AND FLUIDS:

By checking the appropriate line below, I specifically:

_____Authorize the withholding or withdrawal of artificially provided food, water or other nourishment or fluids.

_____DO NOT authorize the withholding or withdrawal of artificially provided food, water or other nourishment or fluids.

ORGAN DONOR CERTIFICATION:

Notwithstanding my previous declaration relative to the withholding or withdrawal of life-prolonging procedures, if as indicated below I have expressed my desire to donate my organs and/or tissues for transplantation, or any of them as specifically designated herein, I do direct my attending physician, if I have been determined dead according to Tennessee Code Annotated, § 68-3-501(b), to maintain me on artificial support systems only for the period of time required to maintain the viability of and to remove such organs and/or tissues.

By checking the appropriate line below, I specifically:

_____Desire to donate my organs and/or tissues for transplantation.

_____Desire to donate my _____
(insert specific organs and/or tissues for transplantation)

_____DO NOT desire to donate my organs or tissues for transplantation.

In the absence of my ability to give directions regarding my medical care, it is my intention that this declaration shall be honored by my family and physician as the final expression of my legal right to refuse medical care and accept the consequences of such refusal.

The definitions of terms used herein shall be as set forth in the Tennessee Right to Natural Death Act, Tennessee Code Annotated, § 32-11-103.

I understand the full import of this declaration, and I am emotionally and mentally competent to make this declaration.

In acknowledgment whereof, I do hereinafter affix my signature on this the _____ day of _____, 200_____.

_____
Declarant

We, the subscribing witnesses hereto, are personally acquainted with and subscribe our names hereto at the request of the declarant, an adult, whom we believe to be of sound mind, fully aware of the action taken herein and its possible consequence.

We, the undersigned witnesses, further declare that we are not related to the declarant by blood or marriage; that we are not entitled to any portion of the estate of the declarant upon the declarant's decease under any will or codicil thereto presently existing or by operation of law then existing; that we are not the attending physician, an employee of the attending physician or, health facility in which the declarant is a patient; and that we are not persons who, at the present time, have a claim against any portion of the estate of the declarant upon the declarant's death.

_____   _____
Witness   Witness

STATE OF TENNESSEE
COUNTY OF _____

Subscribed, sworn to and acknowledged before me by _____, the declarant, and subscribed and sworn to before me by _____ and _____, witnesses, this _____ day of _____, 200_____.

_____
Notary Public

My Commission Expires:_____

DIRECTIVE TO PHYSICIANS AND FAMILY OR SURROGATES

Instructions for completing this document:

This is an important legal document known as an Advance Directive. It is designed to help you communicate your wishes about medical treatment at some time in the future when you are unable to make your wishes known because of illness or injury. These wishes are usually based on personal values. In particular, you may want to consider what burdens or hardships of treatment you would be willing to accept for a particular amount of benefit obtained if you were seriously ill.

You are encouraged to discuss your values and wishes with your family or chosen spokesperson, as well as your physician. Your physician, other health care provider, or medical institution may provide you with various resources to assist you in completing your advance directive. Brief definitions are listed below and may aid you in your discussions and advance planning. Initial the treatment choices that best reflect your personal preferences. Provide a copy of your directive to your physician, usual hospital, and family or spokesperson. Consider a periodic review of this document. By periodic review, you can best assure that the directive reflects your preferences.

In addition to this advance directive, Texas law provides for two other types of directives that can be important during a serious illness. These are the Medical Power of Attorney and the Out-of-Hospital Do-Not-Resuscitate Order. You may wish to discuss these with your physician, family, hospital representative, or other advisers. You may also wish to complete a directive related to the donation of organs and tissues.

DIRECTIVE

I, _____, recognize that the best health care is based upon a partnership of trust and communication with my physician. My physician and I will make health care decisions together as long as I am of sound mind and able to make my wishes known. If there comes a time that I am unable to make medical decisions about myself because of illness or injury, I direct that the following treatment preferences be honored:

If, in the judgment of my physician, I am suffering with a terminal condition from which I am expected to die within six months, even with available life-sustaining treatment provided in accordance with prevailing standards of medical care:

_____   I request that all treatments other than those needed to keep me comfortable be discontinued or withheld and my physician allow me to die as gently as possible; OR

_____ I request that I be kept alive in this terminal condition using available life-sustaining treatment. (THIS SELECTION DOES NOT APPLY TO HOSPICE CARE.)

If, in the judgment of my physician, I am suffering with an irreversible condition so that I cannot care for myself or make decisions for myself and am expected to die without life-sustaining treatment provided in accordance with prevailing standards of care:

_____ I request that all treatments other than those needed to keep me comfortable by discontinued or withheld and my physician allow me to die as gently as possible; OR

_____ I request that I be kept alive in this irreversible condition using available life-sustaining treatment. (THIS SELECTION DOES NOT APPLY TO HOSPICE CARE.)

Additional requests: (After discussion with your physician, you may wish to consider listing particular treatments in this space that you do or do not want in specific circumstances, such as artificial nutrition and fluids, intravenous antibiotics, etc. Be sure to state whether you do or do not want the particular treatment.)

_____

_____

_____

After signing this directive, if my representative or I elect hospice care, I understand and agree that only those treatments needed to keep me comfortable would be provided and I would not be given available life-sustaining treatments.

If I do not have a Medical Power of Attorney, and I am unable to make my wishes known, I designate the following person(s) to make treatment decisions with my physician compatible with my personal values:

1._____

2._____

(If a Medical Power of Attorney has been executed, then an agent already has been named and you should not list additional names in this document.)

If the above persons are not available, or if I have not designated a spokesperson, I understand that a spokesperson will be chosen for me following standards specified in the laws of Texas. If, in the judgment of my physician, my death is imminent within minutes to hours, even with the use of all available medical treatment provided within the prevailing standard of care, I acknowledge that all treatments may be withheld or removed except those needed to maintain my comfort. I understand that under Texas law this directive has no effect if I have been diagnosed as pregnant. This directive will remain in effect until I revoke it. No other person may do so.

Signed _____ Date_____
City, County, State of Residence _____

Two competent adult witnesses must sign below, acknowledging the signature of the declarant. The witness designated as Witness 1 may not be a person designated to make a treatment decision for the patient and may not be related to the patient by blood or marriage. This witness may not be entitled to any part of the estate and may not have a claim against the estate of the patient. This witness may not be the attending physician or an employee of the attending physician. If this witness is an employee of a health care facility in which the patient is being cared for, this witness may not be involved in providing direct patient care to the patient. This witness may not be an officer, director, partner, or business office employee of a health care facility in which the patient is being cared for or of any parent organization of the health care facility.

Witness 1 _____ Witness 2 _____

Definitions:

"Artificial nutrition and hydration" means the provision of nutrients or fluids by a tube inserted in a vein, under the skin in the subcutaneous tissues, or in the stomach (gastrointestinal tract).

"Irreversible condition" means a condition, injury, or illness:

(1) that may be treated, but is never cured or eliminated;

(2) that leaves a person unable to care for or make decisions for the person's own self; and

(3) that, without life-sustaining treatment provided in accordance with the prevailing standard of medical care, is fatal.

Explanation: Many serious illnesses such as cancer, failure of major organs (kidney, heart, liver, or lung), and serious brain disease such as Alzheimer's dementia may be considered irreversible early on. There is no cure, but the patient may be kept alive for prolonged periods of time if the patient receives life-sustaining treatments. Late in the course of the same illness, the disease may be considered terminal when, even with treatment, the patient is expected to die. You may wish to consider which burdens of treatment you would be willing to accept in an effort to achieve a particular outcome. This is a very personal decision that you may wish to discuss with your physician, family, or other important persons in your life.

"Life-sustaining treatment" means treatment that, based on reasonable medical judgment, sustains the life of a patient and without which the patient will die. The term includes both life-sustaining medications and artificial life support such as mechanical breathing machines, kidney dialysis treatment, and artificial hydration and nutrition. The term does not include the administration of pain management medication, the performance of a medical procedure necessary to provide comfort care, or any other medical care provided to alleviate a patient's pain.

"Terminal condition" means an incurable condition caused by injury, disease, or illness that according to reasonable medical judgment will produce death within six months, even with available life-sustaining treatment provided in accordance with the prevailing standard of medical care.

Explanation: Many serious illnesses may be considered irreversible early in the course of the illness, but they may not be considered terminal until the disease is fairly advanced. In thinking about terminal illness and its treatment, you again may wish to consider the relative benefits and burdens of treatment and discuss your wishes with your physician, family, or other important persons in your life.

MEDICAL POWER OF ATTORNEY

INFORMATION CONCERNING THE MEDICAL POWER OF ATTORNEY

THIS IS AN IMPORTANT LEGAL DOCUMENT. BEFORE SIGNING THIS DOCUMENT, YOU SHOULD KNOW THESE IMPORTANT FACTS:

Except to the extent you state otherwise, this document gives the person you name as your agent the authority to make any and all health care decisions for you in accordance with your wishes, including your religious and moral beliefs, when you are no longer capable of making them yourself. Because "health care" means any treatment, service, or procedure to maintain, diagnose, or treat your physical or mental condition, your agent has the power to make a broad range of health care decisions for you. Your agent may consent, refuse to consent, or withdraw consent to medical treatment and may make decisions about withdrawing or withholding life-sustaining treatment. Your agent may not consent to voluntary inpatient mental health services, convulsive treatment, psychosurgery, or abortion. A physician must comply with your agent's instructions or allow you to be transferred to another physician.

Your agent's authority begins when your doctor certifies that you lack the competence to make health care decisions.

Your agent is obligated to follow your instructions when making decisions on your behalf. Unless you state otherwise, your agent has the same authority to make decisions about your health care as you would have had.

It is important that you discuss this document with your physician or other health care provider before you sign it to make sure that you understand the nature and range of decisions that may be made on your behalf. If you do not have a physician, you should talk with someone else who is knowledgeable about these issues and can answer your questions. You do not need a lawyer's assistance to complete this document, but if there is anything in this document that you do not understand, you should ask a lawyer to explain it to you.

The person you appoint as agent should be someone you know and trust. The person must be 18 years of age or older or a person under 18 years of age who has had the disabilities of minority removed. If you appoint your health or residential care provider (e.g., your physician or an employee of a home health agency, hospital, nursing home, or residential care home, other than a relative), that person has to choose between acting as your agent or as your health or residential care provider; the law does not permit a person to do both at the same time.

You should inform the person you appoint that you want the person to be your health care agent. You should discuss this document with your agent and your physician and give each a signed copy. You should indicate on the document itself the people and institutions who have signed copies. Your agent is not liable for health care decisions made in good faith on your behalf.

Even after you have signed this document, you have the right to make health care decisions for yourself as long as you are able to do so and treatment cannot be given to you or stopped over your objection. You have the right to revoke the authority granted to your agent by informing your agent or your health or residential care provider orally or in writing or by your execution of a subsequent medical power of attorney. Unless you state otherwise, your appointment of a spouse dissolves on divorce.

This document may not be changed or modified. If you want to make changes in the document, you must make an entirely new one.

You may wish to designate an alternate agent in the event that your agent is unwilling, unable, or ineligible to act as your agent. Any alternate agent you designate has the same authority to make health care decisions for you.

THIS POWER OF ATTORNEY IS NOT VALID UNLESS IT IS SIGNED IN THE PRESENCE OF TWO COMPETENT ADULT WITNESSES. THE FOLLOWING PERSONS MAY NOT ACT AS ONE OF THE WITNESSES:

(1) the person you have designated as your agent;

(2) a person related to you by blood or marriage;

(3) a person entitled to any part of your estate after your death under a will or codicil executed by you or by operation of law;

(4) your attending physician;

(5) an employee of your attending physician;

(6) an employee of a health care facility in which you are a patient if the employee is providing direct patient care to you or is an officer, director, partner, or business office employee of the health care facility or of any parent organization of the health care facility; or

(7) a person who, at the time this power of attorney is executed, has a claim against any part of your estate after your death.

MEDICAL POWER OF ATTORNEY DESIGNATION OF HEALTH CARE AGENT

I,_____(insert your name) appoint:

Name: _____

Address: _____

Phone: _____

as my agent to make any and all health care decisions for me, except to the extent I state otherwise in this document. This medical power of attorney takes effect if I become unable to make my own health care decisions and this fact is certified in writing by my physician.

LIMITATIONS ON THE DECISION-MAKING AUTHORITY OF MY AGENT ARE AS FOLLOWS:

_____

_____

_____

DESIGNATION OF ALTERNATE AGENT.

(You are not required to designate an alternate agent but you may do so. An alternate agent may make the same health care decisions as the designated agent if the designated agent is unable or unwilling to act as your agent. If the agent designated is your spouse, the designation is automatically revoked by law if your marriage is dissolved.)

If the person designated as my agent is unable or unwilling to make health care decisions for me, I designate the following persons to serve as my agent to make health care decisions for me as authorized by this document, who serve in the following order:

A.   First Alternate Agent

          Name: _____

          Address: _____

          Phone: _____

B.   Second Alternate Agent

        Name: _____

        Address: _____

        Phone: _____

The original of this document is kept at: _____

_____

_____

The following individuals or institutions have signed copies:

        Name: _____

        Address: _____

        Phone: _____

        Name: _____

        Address: _____

        Phone: _____

DURATION.

I understand that this power of attorney exists indefinitely from the date I execute this document unless I establish a shorter time or revoke the power of attorney. If I am unable to make health care decisions for myself when this power of attorney expires, the authority I have granted my agent continues to exist until the time I become able to make health care decisions for myself.

(IF APPLICABLE) This power of attorney ends on the following date:

_____

PRIOR DESIGNATIONS REVOKED.

I revoke any prior medical power of attorney.

ACKNOWLEDGMENT OF DISCLOSURE STATEMENT.

I have been provided with a disclosure statement explaining the effect of this document. I have read and understand that information contained in the disclosure statement.

(YOU MUST DATE AND SIGN THIS POWER OF ATTORNEY.)

I sign my name to this medical power of attorney on _____ day of _____(month, year) at _____

(City and State)

_____

(Signature)

_____

(Printed Name)

STATEMENT OF FIRST WITNESS.

I am not the person appointed as agent by this document. I am not related to the principal by blood or marriage. I would not be entitled to any portion of the principal's estate on the principal's death. I am not the attending physician of the principal or an employee of the attending physician. I have no claim against any portion of the principal's estate on the principal's death. Furthermore, if I am an employee of a health care facility in which the principal is a patient, I am not involved in providing direct patient care to the principal and am not an officer, director, partner, or business office employee of the health care facility or of any parent organization of the health care facility.

Signature: _____

Printed Name: _____   Date: _____

Address: _____

SIGNATURE OF SECOND WITNESS.

Signature: _____

Printed Name: _____   Date: _____

Address: _____

DIRECTIVE TO PHYSICIANS AND PROVIDERS OF MEDICAL SERVICES

(Pursuant to Section 75-2-1104, UCA)

This directive is made this _____ day of _____, 200____.

1.   I, _____, being of sound mind, willfully and voluntarily make known my desire that my life not be artificially prolonged by life-sustaining procedures except as I may otherwise provide in this directive.

2.   I declare that if at any time I should have an injury, disease, or illness, which is certified in writing to be a terminal condition or persistent vegetative state by two physicians who have personally examined me, and in the opinion of those physicians the application of life-sustaining procedures would serve only to unnaturally prolong the moment of my death and to unnaturally postpone or prolong the dying process, I direct that these procedures be withheld or withdrawn and my death be permitted to occur naturally.

3.   I expressly intend this directive to be a final expression of my legal right to refuse medical or surgical treatment and to accept the consequences from this refusal which shall remain in effect notwithstanding my future inability to give current medical directions to treating physicians and other providers of medical services.

4.   I understand that the term "life-sustaining procedure" includes artificial nutrition and hydration and any other procedures that I specify below to be considered life-sustaining but does not include the administration of medication or the performance of any medical procedure which is intended to provide comfort care or to alleviate pain:_____

5.   I reserve the right to give current medical directions to physicians and other providers of medical services so long as I am able, even though these directions may conflict with the above written directive that life-sustaining procedures be withheld or withdrawn.

6.   I understand the full import of this directive and declare that I am emotionally and mentally competent to make this directive.

_____   _____
Declarant's signature   City, County, and State of Residence

We witnesses certify that each of us is 18 years of age or older and each personally witnessed the declarant sign or direct the signing of this directive; that we are acquainted with the declarant and believe him to be of sound mind; that the declarant's desires are as expressed above; that neither of us is a person who signed the above directive on behalf of the declarant; that we are not related to the declarant by blood or marriage nor are we entitled to any portion of declarant's estate according to the laws of intestate succession of this state or under any will or codicil of declarant; that we are not directly financially responsible for declarant's medical care; and that we are not agents of any health care facility in which the declarant may be a patient at the time of signing this directive.

_____   _____
Signature of Witness   Signature of Witness

_____   _____

TERMINAL CARE DOCUMENT

To my family, my physician, my lawyer, my clergyman. To any medical facility in whose care I happen to be. To any individual who may become responsible for my health, welfare or affairs.

Death is as much a reality as birth, growth, maturity and old age—it is the one certainty of life. If the time comes when I, _____, can no longer take part in decisions of my own future, let this statement stand as an expression of my wishes, while I am still of sound mind.

If the situation should arise in which I am in a terminal state and there is no reasonable expectation of my recovery, I direct that I be allowed to die a natural death and that my life not be prolonged by extraordinary measures. I do, however, ask that medication be mercifully administered to me to alleviate suffering even though this may shorten my remaining life.

This statement is made after careful consideration and is in accordance with my strong convictions and beliefs. I want the wishes and directions here expressed carried out to the extent permitted by law. Insofar as they are not legally enforceable, I hope that those to whom this will is addressed will regard themselves as morally bound by these provisions.

Signed:_____

Date:_____

Witness:_____

Witness:_____

Copies of this request have been given to:

_____

_____

_____

ADVANCE MEDICAL DIRECTIVE

I, _____, willfully and voluntarily make known my desire and hereby declare:

If at any time my attending physician should determine that I have a terminal condition where the application of life-prolonging procedures would serve only to artificially prolong the dying process, I direct that such procedures be withheld or withdrawn, and that I be permitted to die naturally with only the administration of medication or the performance of any medical procedure deemed necessary to provide me with comfort care or to alleviate pain (OPTION: I specifically direct that the following procedures or treatments be provided to me:

_____
_____)

In the absence of my ability to give directions regarding the use of such life-prolonging procedures, it is my intention that this advance directive shall be honored by my family and physician as the final expression of my legal right to refuse medical or surgical treatment and accept the consequences of such refusal.

OPTION: APPOINTMENT OF AGENT (CROSS THROUGH IF YOU DO NOT WANT TO APPOINT AN AGENT TO MAKE HEALTH CARE DECISIONS FOR YOU.)

I hereby appoint _____ (primary agent), of _____
_____ (address and telephone number), as my agent to make health care decisions on my behalf as authorized in this document. If _____
_____ (primary agent) is not reasonably available or is unable or unwilling to act as my agent, then I appoint _____ (successor agent), of _____
_____ (address and telephone number), to serve in that capacity.

I hereby grant to my agent, named above, full power and authority to make health care decisions on my behalf as described below whenever I have been determined to be incapable of making an informed decision about providing, withholding or withdrawing, medical treatment. The phrase "incapable of making an informed decision" means unable to understand the nature, extent and probably consequences of a proposed medical decision or unable to make a rational evaluation of the risks and benefits of a proposed medical decision as compared with the risks and benefits of alternatives to that decision, or unable to communicate such understanding in any way. My agent's authority hereunder is effective as long as I am incapable of making an informed decision.

The determination that I am incapable of making an informed decision shall be made by my attending physician and a second physician or licensed clinical psychologist after a personal examination of me and shall be certified in writing. Such certification shall be required before treatment is withheld or withdrawn, and before, or as soon as reasonably practicable after, treatment is provided, and every 180 days thereafter while the treatment continues.

In exercising the power to make health care decisions on my behalf, my agent shall follow my desires and preferences as stated in this document or as otherwise known to my agent. My agent shall be guided by my medical diagnosis and prognosis and any information provided by my physicians as to the intrusiveness, pain, risks, and side effects associated with treatment or nontreatment. My agent shall not authorize a course of treatment which he knows, or upon reasonable inquiry ought to know, is contrary to my religious beliefs or my basic values, whether expressed orally or in writing. If my agent cannot determine what treatment choice I would have made on my own behalf, then my agent shall make a choice for me based upon what he believes to be in my best interests.

OPTION: POWERS OF MY AGENT (CROSS THROUGH ANY LANGUAGE YOU DO NOT WANT AND ADD ANY LANGUAGE YOU DO WANT.)

The powers of my agent shall include the following:

A. To consent to or refuse or withdraw consent to any type of medical care, treatment, surgical procedure, diagnostic procedure, medication and the use of mechanical or other procedures that affect any bodily function, including, but not limited to , artificial respiration, artificially administered nutrition and hydration, and cardiopulmonary resuscitation. This authorization specifically includes the power to consent to the administration of dosages of pain relieving medication in excess of standard doses in an amount sufficient to relieve pain, even if such medication carries the risk of addiction or inadvertently hastens my death;

B. To request, receive, and review any information, verbal or written, regarding my physical or mental health, including, but not limited to, medical and hospital records, and to consent to the disclosure of this information;

C. To employ and discharge my health care providers;

D. To authorize my admission to or discharge (including transfer to another facility) from any hospital, hospice, nursing home, adult home or other medical care facility; and

E. To take any lawful actions that may be necessary to carry out these decisions, including the granting of releases of liability to medical providers.

Further, my agent shall not be liable for the costs of treatment pursuant to his authorization, based solely on that authorization.

OPTION: APPOINTMENT OF AN AGENT TO MAKE AN ANATOMICAL GIFT (CROSS THROUGH IF YOU DO NOT WANT TO APPOINT AN AGENT TO MAKE AN ANATOMICAL GIFT FOR YOU.)

Upon my death, I direct that an anatomical gift of all or part of my body be made pursuant to Article 2 (§ 32.1-289 et seq.) of Chapter 8 of Title 32.1 and in accordance with my directions, if any. I hereby appoint
_____ as my agent, of
_____
_____ (address and telephone number), to make any such anatomical gift following my death.
I further direct that _____
_____
_____
_____
_____ (declarant's directions concerning anatomical gift).

This advance directive shall not terminate in the event of my disability.

By signing below, I indicate that I am emotionally and mentally competent to make this advance directive and that I understand the purpose and effect of this document.

_____   _____

(Date)   (Signature of Declarant)

The declarant signed the foregoing advance directive in my presence. I am not the spouse or a blood relative of the declarant.

(Witness) _____   (Witness) _____

HEALTH CARE DIRECTIVE

Directive made this _____ day of _____ (month, year).

I, _____, having the capacity to make health care decisions, willfully, and voluntarily make known my desire that my dying shall not be artificially prolonged under the circumstances set forth below, and do hereby declare that:

(a) If at any time I should be diagnosed in writing to be in a terminal condition by the attending physician, or in a permanent unconscious condition by two physicians, and where the application of life-sustaining treatment would serve only to artificially prolong the process of my dying, I direct that such treatment be withheld or withdrawn, and that I be permitted to die naturally. I understand by using this form that a terminal condition means an incurable and irreversible condition caused by injury, disease, or illness, that would within reasonable medical judgment cause death within a reasonable period of time in accordance with accepted medical standards, and where the application of life-sustaining treatment would serve only to prolong the process of dying. I further understand in using this form that a permanent unconscious condition means an incurable and irreversible condition in which I am medically assess within reasonable medical judgment as having no reasonable probability of recovery from an irreversible coma or a persistent vegetative state.

(b) In the absence of my ability to give directions regarding the use of such life-sustaining treatment, it is my intention that this directive shall be honored by my family and physician(s) as the final expression of my legal right to refuse medical or surgical treatment and I accept the consequences of such refusal. If another person is appointed to make these decisions for me, whether through a durable power of attorney or otherwise, I request that the person be guided by this directive and any other clear expressions of my desires.

(c) If I am diagnosed to be in a terminal condition or a permanent unconscious condition (check one):
_____ I DO want to have artificially provided nutrition and hydration.
_____ I DO NOT want to have artificially provided nutrition and hydration.

(d) If I have been diagnosed as pregnant and that diagnosis is known to my physician, this directive shall have no force or effect during the course of my pregnancy.

(e) I understand the full import of this directive and I am emotionally and mentally capable to make the health care decisions contained in this directive.

(f) I understand that before I sign this directive, I can add to or delete from or otherwise change the wording of this directive and that I may add to or delete from this directive at any time and that any changes shall be consistent with Washington state law or federal constitutional law to be legally valid.

(g) It is my wish that every part of this directive be fully implemented. If for any reason any part is held invalid it is my wish that the remainder of my directive be implemented.

Signed_____

_____
City, County, and State of Residence

The declarer has been personally known to me and I believe him or her to be capable of making health care decisions.

Witness_____

Witness_____

STATE OF WEST VIRGINIA
LIVING WILL

Living will made this _____day of _____(month, year).

I,_____, being of sound mind, willfully and voluntarily declare that I want my wishes to be respected if I am very sick and not able to communicate my wishes for myself. In the absence of my ability to give directions regarding the use of life-prolonging medical intervention, it is my desire that my dying shall not be prolonged under the following circumstances:

If I am very sick and not able to communicate my wishes for myself and I am certified by one physician, who has personally examined me, to have a terminal condition or to be in a persistent vegetative state (I am unconscious and am neither aware of my environment nor able to interact with others), I direct that life-prolonging medical intervention that would serve solely to prolong the dying process or maintain me in a persistent vegetative state be withheld or withdrawn. I want to be allowed to die naturally and only be given medications or other medical procedures necessary to keep me comfortable. I want to receive as much medication as is necessary to alleviate my pain.

I give the following SPECIAL DIRECTIVES OR LIMITATIONS: (Comments about tube feedings, breathing machines, cardiopulmonary resuscitation, dialysis and mental health treatment may be placed here. My failure to provide special directives or limitations does not mean that I want or refuse certain treatments.) _____

_____

_____

It is my intention that this living will be honored as the final expression of my legal right to refuse medical or surgical treatment and accept the consequences resulting from such refusal.

I understand the full import of this living will.

_____

Signed

_____

Address

I did not sign the principal's signature above for or at the direction of the principal. I am at least eighteen years of age and am not related to the principal by blood or marriage, entitled to any portion of the estate of the principal to the best of my knowledge under any will of principal or codicil thereto, or directly financially responsible for principal's medical care. I am not the principal's attending physician or the principal's medical power of attorney representative or successor medical power of attorney representative under a medical power of attorney.

_____   _____

Witness   Date

_____   _____

Witness   Date

_____

STATE OF

_____

COUNTY OF

I, _____, a Notary Public of said County, do certify that
_____, as principal, and_____
and _____, as witnesses, whose names are signed to the writing above
bearing date on the _____ day of _____, 20____,have this day acknowledged the same before me.
Given under my hand this _____ day of _____, 20____.
My commission expires:_____

_____

Notary Public

STATE OF WEST VIRGINIA
MEDICAL POWER OF ATTORNEY

Dated: _____ , 20_____

I, _____ , hereby
        (Insert your name and address)

appoint my representative to act on my behalf to give, withhold or withdraw informed consent to
health care decisions in the event that I am not able to do so myself.

The person I choose as my representative is:

_____

(Insert the name, address, area code and telephone number of the person you wish to designate as
your representative)

The person I choose as my successor representative is:

If my representative is unable, unwilling or disqualified to serve, then I appoint:

_____

(Insert the name, address, area code and telephone number of the person you wish to designate as
your successor representative)

This appointment shall extend to, but not be limited to, health care decisions relating to medical treatment, surgical treatment, nursing care, medication, hospitalization, care and treatment in a
nursing home or other facility, and home health care. The representative appointed by this document
is specifically authorized to be granted access to my medical records and other health information and
to act on my behalf to consent to, refuse or withdraw any and all medical treatment or diagnostic procedures, or autopsy if my representative determines that I, if able to do so, would consent to, refuse
or withdraw such treatment or procedures. Such authority shall include, but not be limited to, decisions regarding the withholding or withdrawal of life-prolonging interventions.

I appoint this representative because I believe this person understands my wishes and values
and will act to carry into effect the health care decisions that I would make if I were able to do so and
because I also believe that this person will act in my best interest when my wishes are unknown. It is
my intent that my family, my physician and all legal authorities be bound by the decisions that are
made by the representative appointed by this document and it is my intent that these decisions should
not be the subject of review by any health care provider or administrative or judicial agency.

It is my intent that this document be legally binding and effective and that this document be
taken as a formal statement of my desire concerning the method by which any health care decisions
should be made on my behalf during any period when I am unable to make such decisions.

In exercising the authority under this medical power of attorney, my representative shall act consistently with my special directives or limitations as stated below.

I am giving the following SPECIAL DIRECTIVES OR LIMITATIONS ON THIS POWER: (Comments about tube feedings, breathing machines, cardiopulmonary resuscitation, dialysis, funeral arrangements, autopsy and organ donation may be placed here. My failure to provide special directives or limitations does not mean that I want or refuse certain treatments.)

_____

_____

THIS MEDICAL POWER OF ATTORNEY SHALL BECOME EFFECTIVE ONLY UPON MY INCAPACITY TO GIVE, WITHHOLD OR WITHDRAW INFORMED CONSENT TO MY OWN MEDICAL CARE.

_____

Signature of the Principal

I did not sign the principal's signature above. I am at least eighteen years of age and am not related to the principal by blood or marriage. I am not entitled to any portion of the estate of the principal or to the best of my knowledge under any will of the principal or codicil thereto, or legally responsible for the costs of the principal's medical or other care. I am not the principal's attending physician, nor am I the representative or successor representative of the principal.

_____

_____   _____
Witness   Date

_____   _____
Witness   Date

_____
STATE OF

_____
COUNTY OF

I, _____, a Notary Public of said County, do certify that_____, as principal, and _____ and _____, as witnesses, whose names are signed to the writing above bearing date on the _____ day of _____, 20_____, have this day acknowledged the same before me.
Given under my hand this _____ day of _____, 20_____.
My commission expires:_____

_____
Notary Public

DECLARATION TO PHYSICIANS

I, _____, being of sound mind, voluntarily state my desire that my dying may not be prolonged under the circumstances specified in this document. Under those circumstances, I direct that I be permitted to die naturally. If I am unable to give directions regarding the use of life-sustaining procedures or feeding tubes, I intend that my family and physician honor this document as the final expression of my legal right to refuse medical or surgical treatment.

1. If I have a TERMINAL CONDITION, as determined by 2 physicians who have personally examined me, I do not want my dying to be artificially prolonged and I do not want life-sustaining procedures to be used. In addition, the following are my directions regarding the use of feeding tubes (check only one):

___ YES, I want feeding tubes used if I have a terminal condition.
___ NO, I do not want feeding tubes used if I have a terminal condition.
If you have not checked either box, feeding tubes will be used.

2. If I am in a PERSISTENT VEGETATIVE STATE, as determined by 2 physicians who have personally examined me, the following are my directions regarding the use of life-sustaining procedures:

___ YES, I want life-sustaining procedures used if I am in a persistent vegetative state.
___ NO, I do not want life-sustaining procedures used if I am in a persistent vegetative state.
If you have not checked either box, life-sustaining procedures will be used.

3. If I am in a PERSISTENT VEGETATIVE STATE, as determined by 2 physicians who have personally examined me, the following are my directions regarding the use of feeding tubes:
___ YES, I want feeding tubes used if I am in a persistent vegetative state.
___ NO, I do not want feeding tubes used if I am in a persistent vegetative state.
If you have not checked either box, feeding tubes will be used.

If you are interested in more information about the significant terms used in this document, see section 154.01 of the Wisconsin Statutes or the information accompanying this document.

ATTENTION: You and the 2 witnesses must sign the document at the same time.

Signed _____   Date _____

Address _____   Date of birth _____

_____

I believe that the person signing this document is of sound mind. I am an adult and am not related to the person signing this document by blood, marriage, or adoption. I am not entitled to and do not have a claim on any portion of the person's estate and am not otherwise restricted by law from being a witness.

Witness signature _____ Date signed _____

Print name _____

Witness signature _____ Date signed _____

Print name _____

DIRECTIVES TO ATTENDING PHYSICIAN

1.   This document authorizes the withholding or withdrawal of life-sustaining procedures or of feeding tubes when 2 physicians, one of whom is the attending physician, have personally examined and certified in writing that the patient has a terminal condition or is in a persistent vegetative state.

2.   The choices in this document were made by a competent adult. Under the law, the patient's stated desires must be followed unless you believe that withholding or withdrawing life-sustaining procedures or feeding tubes would cause the patient pain or reduced comfort and that the pain or discomfort cannot be alleviated through pain relief measures. If the patient's stated desires are that life-sustaining procedures or feeding tubes be used, this directive must be followed.

3.   If you feel that you cannot comply with this document, you must make a good faith attempt to transfer the patient to another physician who will comply. Refusal or failure to make a good faith attempt to do so constitutes unprofessional conduct.

4.   If you know that the patient is pregnant, this document has no effect during her pregnancy.

* * * * *

The person making this living will may use the following space to record the names of those individuals and health care providers to whom he or she has given copies of this document:

_____
_____
_____
_____

DECLARATION

NOTICE

This document has significant medical, legal and possible ethical implications and effects. Before you sign this document, you should become completely familiar with these implications and effects. The operation, effects and implications of this document may be discussed with a physician, a lawyer and a clergyman of your choice.

Declaration made this _____ day of _____ (month, year). I, _____, being of sound mind, willfully and voluntarily make known my desire that my dying shall not be artificially prolonged under the circumstances set forth below, do hereby declare:

If at any time I should have an incurable injury, disease or other illness certified to be a terminal condition by two (2) physicians who have personally examined me, one (1) of whom shall be my attending physician, and the physicians have determined that my death will occur whether or not life-sustaining procedures are utilized and where the application of life-sustaining procedures would serve only to artificially prolong the dying process, I direct that such procedures be withheld or withdrawn, and that I be permitted to die naturally with only the administration of medication or the performance of any medical procedure deemed necessary to provide me with comfort care.

If, in spite of this declaration, I am comatose or otherwise unable to make treatment decisions for myself, I HEREBY designate _____ to make treatment decisions for me.

In the absence of my ability to give directions regarding the use of life-sustaining procedures, it is my intention that this declaration shall be honored by my family and physician(s) and agent as the final expression of my legal right to refuse medical or surgical treatment and accept the consequences from this refusal. I understand the full import or this declaration and I am emotionally and mentally competent to make this declaration.

Signed_____

City, County and State of Residence_____

The declarant has been personally known to me and I believe him or her to be of sound mind. I did not sign the declarant's signature above for or at the direction of the declarant. I am not related to the declarant by blood or marriage, entitled to any portion of the estate of the declarant according to the laws of intestate succession or under any will of the declarant or codicil thereto, or directly financially responsible for declarant's medical care.

Witness_____

Witness_____

STATEMENT OF DESIRES AND LOCATION OF PROPERTY & DOCUMENTS

I, _____, am signing this document as the expression of my desires as to the matters stated below, and to inform my family members or other significant persons of the location of certain property and documents in the event of any emergency or of my death.

1. **Funeral Desires.** It is my desire that the following arrangements be made for my funeral and disposition of remains in the event of my death (state if you have made any arrangements, such as pre-paid burial plans, cemetery plots owned, etc.):

    ☐ Burial at _____

    _____.

    ☐ Cremation at _____

    _____.

    ☐ Other specific desires: _____

    _____

    _____.

2. **Minor Children.** I have the following minor child(ren): _____

    _____. The following are my desires concerning the custody, education, and rearing of said minor child(ren): _____

    _____

    _____

    _____

    _____

    _____.

3. **Pets.** I have the following pet(s): _____

    _____. The following are my desires concerning the care of said pet(s): _____

    _____

    _____.

4. **Notification.** I would like the following person(s) notified in the event of emergency or death (give name, address and phone number):

    _____

    _____

    _____

    _____

    _____.

5. **Location of Documents.** The following is a list of important documents, and their location:

☐ Last Will and Testament, dated _____. Location: _____

_____.

☐ Durable Power of Attorney, dated _____. Location: _____

_____.

☐ Living Will, dated _____. Location: _____

_____.

☐ Deed(s) to real estate (describe property location and location of deed):

_____

_____

_____

☐ Title(s) to vehicles (cars, boats, etc.) (Describe vehicle, its location, and location of title, registration, or other documents):

_____

_____

_____

_____

☐ Life insurance policies (list name address & phone number of insurance company and insurance agent, policy number, and location of policy):

_____

_____

_____

☐ Other insurance policies (list type, company & agent, policy number, and location of policy):

_____

_____

_____

_____

_____

☐ Other: (list other documents such as stock certificates, bonds, certificates of deposit, etc., and their location):

_____

_____

_____

_____

6. **Location of Assets.** In addition to items readily visible in my home or listed above, I have the following assets:

☐ Safe deposit box located at _____, box number _____.

   Key located at: _____.

☐ Bank accounts (list name & address of bank, type of account, and account number):

_____

☐ Other (describe the item and give its location):

_____

_____

_____

_____

_____

_____

7. Other desires or information (state any desires or provide any information not given above; use additional sheets of paper if necessary):

_____

_____

_____

_____

_____

Dated: _____

_____
Signature

STANDARD NOTARY PAGE

State of _____   )

County of _____   )

    On this _____ day of _____, 200_____, before me, personally appeared _____, principal, and _____ and _____, witnesses, who are personally known to me or who provided _____ _____ as identification, and signed the foregoing instrument in my presence.

_____
Notary Public

My Commission expires:

ADDENDUM TO LIVING WILL

I, _____, hereby execute this addendum to the
_____ ("my living will"), exe-
cuted by me on _____, 200____. The sole purpose of this addendum is to more
fully express my wishes regarding my medical treatment. If any or all of the terms of this addendum are determined to be invalid, my living will shall remain in effect. My desires regarding my medical care and treatment
are as indicated below:

_____ 1. If I should have an incurable or irreversible condition that will cause my death within a relatively short time without the administration of artificial life support procedures or treatment, and
if I am unable to make decisions regarding my medical treatment, I direct my attending physician to withhold or withdraw procedures that merely prolong the dying process and are not
necessary to my comfort or to alleviate pain. This authorization includes, but is not limited to,
the withholding or withdrawal of the following types of medical treatment (subject to any special
instructions in paragraph 5 below):

_____ a. Artificial feeding and hydration.
_____ b. Cardiopulmonary resuscitation (this includes, but is not limited to, the use
of drugs, electric shock, and artificial breathing).
_____ c. Kidney dialysis.
_____ d. Surgery or other invasive procedures.
_____ e. Drugs and antibiotics.
_____ f. Transfusions of blood or blood products.
_____ g. Other: _____
_____

_____ 2. If I should be in an irreversible coma or persistent vegetative state that my physician reasonably believes to be irreversible or incurable, I direct my attending physician to withhold or
withdraw medical procedures and treatment other than such medical procedures and treatment necessary to my comfort or to alleviate pain. This authorization includes, but is not limited
to, the withholding or withdrawal of the following types of medical treatment (subject to any special instructions in paragraph 5 below):

_____ a. Artificial feeding and hydration.
_____ b. Cardiopulmonary resuscitation (this includes, but is not limited to, the use
of drugs, electric shock, and artificial breathing).
_____ c. Kidney dialysis.
_____ d. Surgery or other invasive procedures.
_____ e. Drugs and antibiotics.
_____ f. Transfusions of blood or blood products.
_____ g. Other: _____
_____

_____ 3. If I should have a medical condition where I am unable to communicate my desires as to
treatment and my physician determines that the burdens of treatment outweigh the expected
benefits, I direct my attending physician to withhold or withdraw medical procedures and
treatment other than such medical procedures and treatment necessary to my comfort or to
alleviate pain. This authorization includes, but is not limited to, the withholding or withdrawal of the following types of medical treatment (subject to any special instructions in
paragraph 5 below):

_____ a. Artificial feeding and hydration.

_____ b. Cardiopulmonary resuscitation (this includes, but is not limited to, the use of drugs, electric shock, and artificial breathing).

_____ c. Kidney dialysis.

_____ d. Surgery or other invasive procedures.

_____ e. Drugs and antibiotics.

_____ f. Transfusions of blood or blood products.

_____ g. Other: _____

_____

_____ 4. I want my life prolonged to the greatest extent possible (subject to any special instructions in paragraph 5 below).

_____ 5. Special instructions (if any) _____

_____

_____

_____

Signed this _____ day of _____, 200____.

_____
Signature

Address:_____

_____

Each of the undersigned hereby witnesses the forgoing signature of the declarant, and attests that the declarant is personally known to me, that I believe the declarant to be of sound mind, and that the declarant voluntarily signed this document in my presence. I further attest that I am at least 18 years of age; that I am not related to the declarant by blood, marriage, or adoption; that I do not have a claim against any portion of the estate of the declarant; that I am not entitled to any portion of the declarant's estate by any will or codicil or by operation of law; that I am not the attending physician, nor an employee of the attending physician, of the declarant; that I am not employed by, an agent of, or a patient in, a health facility in which the declarant is a patient; that I am not directly responsible for the financial affairs or medical care of the declarant; that I did not sign this document on behalf of the declarant; and that I am not the declarant's health care representative or successor health care representative under a health care power of attorney.

Witness:_____   Witness_____

Name:_____   Name:_____

Address:_____   Address:_____

DURABLE POWER OF ATTORNEY FOR HEALTH CARE

1. Appointment of Agent. I, _____, appoint
_____, as my agent for health care decisions (called "Agent" in
the rest of this document). If my Agent shall be unable or unwilling to make decisions pursuant to this Durable Power
of Attorney for Health Care, I appoint as my alternate Agent _____.

2. Effective Date and Durability. My Agent may only act if I am unable to participate in making decisions
regarding my medical treatment. My attending physician and another physician or licensed psychologist shall determine,
after examining me, when I am unable to participate in making my own medical decisions. This designation is suspended
during any period when I regain the ability to participate in my own medical treatment decisions. I intend this document to be a Durable Power of Attorney for Health Care and it shall survive my disability or incapacity.

3. Agent's Powers. I grant my Agent full authority to make decisions for me. In making such decisions, he or
she should follow my expressed wishes, either written or oral, regarding my medical treatment. If my Agent cannot
determine the choice I would want based on my written or oral statements, then he or she shall choose for me based on
what he or she believes to be in my best interests. I direct that my Agent comply with the following instructions or lim-
itations:_____
_____.

4. Life-sustaining Treatment. (CHOOSE ONLY ONE.) I understand that I do not have to choose any of the
instructions regarding life-sustaining treatment listed below. If I choose one, I will place a check mark by the choice and
sign below my choice. If I sign one of the choices listed below, I direct that reasonable measures be taken to keep me
comfortable and to relieve pain.

[ ] **CHOICE 1:** Life-sustaining treatment: I grant discretion to my Agent.

I do not want life-sustaining treatment ([ ] including artificial delivery of food and water [ ] except for artificial
delivery of food and water) if any of the following medical conditions exist:

   a.   I am in an irreversible coma or persistent vegetative state.

   b.   I am terminally ill, and life-sustaining procedures would only serve to artificially delay my death.

   c.   My medical condition is such that burdens of treatment outweigh the expected benefits. In making this determination, I want my Patient Advocate to consider relief of my suffering, the expenses involved, and the quality
of life, if prolonged.

I expressly authorize my Agent to make decisions to withhold or withdraw treatment which would allow me to die,
and I acknowledge such decisions could or would allow my death.

Signed: _____

OR

[ ] **CHOICE 2:** Life-sustaining treatment: withhold treatment only if I am in a coma or persistent vegetative state.

I want life-sustaining treatment ([ ] including artificial delivery of food and water [ ] except for artificial delivery
of food and water) unless I am in a coma or persistent vegetative state that my physician reasonably believes to be irreversible. Once my physician has reasonably concluded the I will remain unconscious for the rest of my life, I do not want
life sustaining treatment to be provided or continued.

I expressly authorize my Agent to make decisions to withhold or withdraw treatment which would allow me to die,
and I acknowledge such decisions could or would allow my death.

Signed: _____

OR

[ ] **CHOICE 3:** Directive for maximum treatment.

I want my life to be prolonged to the greatest extent possible consistent with sound medical practice without regard
to my condition, the chances I have for recovery, or the cost of the procedures, and I direct life-sustaining treatment to
be provided in order to prolong my life.

Signed: _____

5. Protection of third parties who rely on the instructions of my Agent. No person or entity that relies in good
faith on the instructions of my Agent pursuant to this document, without actual notice that this power has been revoked

or amended, shall incur any liability to me or to my estate. If I am unable to participate in making decisions for my care and there is no Agent to act for me, I request that the instructions I have given in this document be followed and be considered conclusive evidence of my wishes.

6.   Administrative provisions.

I revoke any prior durable powers of attorney for health care that I may have executed to the extent that, and only to the extent that, they grant powers and authority within the scope of the powers granted to the Agent appointed in this document.

The document shall be governed by _____ law. However, I intend for this durable power of attorney for health care to be honored in any jurisdiction where it is presented and for such jurisdiction to refer to _____ law to interpret and determine the validity and enforceability of this document.

Photocopies of this signed power of attorney shall be treated as original counterparts.

I am providing these instructions voluntarily and have not been required to give them to obtain treatment or to have care withheld or withdrawn. I am at least eighteen years of age and of solid mind.

Dated:_____

_____
       Signature

WITNESS STATEMENT

I declare that the person who signed this Durable Power of Attorney for Health Care did so in my presence and appears to be of sound mind and under no duress, fraud or undue influence. I am not the husband or wife, parent, child, grandchild, brother or sister of the person who signed this document. Further, I am not his or her presumptive heir and , to the best of my knowledge, I am not a beneficiary to his or her will at the time of witnessing. I am not the Agent, the physician or an employee of the life or health insurance provider for the person signing this document. Nor am I an employee of the health care facility or home for the aged where the person signing this document resides or is being treated.

Dated:_____   _____
                                                (Signature)

Name: _____
Address: _____
          _____

Dated:_____   _____
                                                (Signature)

Name: _____
Address: _____
          _____

State of _____)
County of _____)

On this _____ day of _____, _____, before me personally appeared _____, principal, and _____ and _____, witnesses, who are personally known to me or who produced _____ as identification, and signed the foregoing instrument in my presence.

_____
Notary Public
My Commission Expires:

Affidavit of Attorney in Fact

STATE OF_____

COUNTY OF_____

Before me, the undersigned authority, personally appeared _____ ("Affiant"), who swore or affirmed that:

1. Affiant is the attorney in fact named in the _____ (title of document) executed by _____ ("Principal") on _____ (date).

2. This _____ (title of document) is currently exercisable by Affiant. The principal is domiciled in _____ (insert name of state, territory, or foreign country).

3. To the best of the Affiant's knowledge after diligent search and inquiry:

   a. The Principal is not deceased; and

   b. The Principal has not partially nor completely revoked or suspended the _____ (title of document); and

   c. There has been no partial or complete termination by adjudication of incapacity or incompetence, by the occurrence of an event referenced in the _____ (title of document), nor any suspension by initiation of proceedings to determine incapacity or to appoint a guardian.

4. Affiant agrees not to exercise any powers granted by the _____ (title of document) if Affiant attains knowledge that it has been partially or completely revoked, terminated, or suspended; or is no longer valid because of the death or adjudication of incapacity or incompetence of the Principal.

_____
(Affiant)

Sworn to (or affirmed) and subscribed before me this _____ day of _____, 20___, by _____ (name of person making statement).

INDEX

Sphinx® Publishing's National Titles
Valid in All 50 States

LEGAL SURVIVAL IN BUSINESS

The Complete Book of Corporate Forms	$24.95
The Complete Partnership Book	$24.95
The Complete Patent Book	$26.95
Employees' Rights	$18.95
Employer's Rights	$24.95
The Entrepreneur's Internet Handbook	$21.95
The Entrepreneur's Legal Guide	$26.95
How to Form a Limited Liability Company (2E)	$24.95
How to Form a Nonprofit Corporation (2E)	$24.95
How to Form Your Own Corporation (4E)	$26.95
How to Register Your Own Copyright (4E)	$24.95
How to Register Your Own Trademark (3E)	$21.95
Incorporate in Delaware from Any State	$24.95
Incorporate in Nevada from Any State	$24.95
The Law (In Plain English)® for Small Business	$19.95
Most Valuable Business Legal Forms You'll Ever Need (3E)	$21.95
Profit from Intellectual Property	$28.95
Protect Your Patent	$24.95
The Small Business Owner's Guide to Bankruptcy	$21.95
Tax Smarts for Small Business	$21.95

LEGAL SURVIVAL IN COURT

Attorney Responsibilities & Client Rights	$19.95
Crime Victim's Guide to Justice (2E)	$21.95
Grandparents' Rights (3E)	$24.95
Help Your Lawyer Win Your Case (2E)	$14.95
Jurors' Rights (2E)	$12.95
Legal Research Made Easy (3E)	$21.95
Winning Your Personal Injury Claim (2E)	$24.95
Your Rights When You Owe Too Much	$16.95

LEGAL SURVIVAL IN REAL ESTATE

The Complete Kit to Selling Your Own Home	$18.95
Essential Guide to Real Estate Contracts (2E)	$18.95
Essential Guide to Real Estate Leases	$18.95
Homeowner's Rights	$19.95
How to Buy a Condominium or Townhome (2E)	$19.95
How to Buy Your First Home	$18.95
Working with Your Homeowners Association	$19.95

LEGAL SURVIVAL IN SPANISH

Cómo Hacer su Propio Testamento	$16.95
Cómo Restablecer su propio Crédito y Renegociar sus Deudas	$21.95
Cómo Solicitar su Propio Divorcio	$24.95
Guía de Inmigración a Estados Unidos (3E)	$24.95
Guía de Justicia para Víctimas del Crimen	$21.95
Guía Esencial para los Contratos de Arrendamiento de Bienes Raices	$22.95
Inmigración a los EE. UU. Paso a Paso	$22.95
Manual de Beneficios para el Seguro Social	$18.95
El Seguro Social Preguntas y Respuestas	$14.95

LEGAL SURVIVAL IN PERSONAL AFFAIRS

101 Complaint Letters That Get Results	$18.95
The 529 College Savings Plan (2E)	$18.95
The Antique and Art Collector's Legal Guide	$24.95
The Complete Legal Guide to Senior Care	$21.95
Credit Smart	$18.95
Family Limited Partnership	$26.95
Gay & Lesbian Rights	$26.95
How to File Your Own Bankruptcy (5E)	$21.95
How to File Your Own Divorce (5E)	$26.95
How to Make Your Own Simple Will (3E)	$18.95
How to Write Your Own Living Will (3E)	$18.95
How to Write Your Own Premarital Agreement (3E)	$24.95
Law School 101	$16.95
Living Trusts and Other Ways to Avoid Probate (3E)	$24.95
Mastering the MBE	$16.95
Most Valuable Personal Legal Forms You'll Ever Need (2E)	$26.95
Neighbor v. Neighbor (2E)	$16.95
The Nanny and Domestic Help Legal Kit	$22.95
The Power of Attorney Handbook (5E)	$22.95
Quick Cash	$14.95
Repair Your Own Credit and Deal with Debt (2E)	$18.95
Sexual Harassment:Your Guide to Legal Action	$18.95
The Social Security Benefits Handbook (3E)	$18.95
Social Security Q&A	$12.95
Teen Rights	$22.95
Traveler's Rights	$21.95
Unmarried Parents' Rights (2E)	$19.95
U.S. Immigration and Citizenship Q&A	$16.95
U.S. Immigration Step by Step (2E)	$24.95
U.S.A. Immigration Guide (5E)	$26.95
The Visitation Handbook	$18.95
The Wills, Estate Planning and Trusts Legal Kit	$26.95
Win Your Unemployment Compensation Claim (2E)	$21.95
Your Right to Child Custody, Visitation and Support (3E)	$24.95

SPHINX® PUBLISHING ORDER FORM

Qty	ISBN	Title	Retail	Ext.	Qty	ISBN	Title	Retail	Ext.
		SPHINX PUBLISHING NATIONAL TITLES				1-57248-377-6	The Law (In Plain English)® for Small Business	$19.95	
	1-57248-363-6	101 Complaint Letters That Get Results	$18.95			1-57248-223-0	Legal Research Made Easy (3E)	$21.95	
	1-57248-361-X	The 529 College Savings Plan (2E)	$18.95			1-57248-165-X	Living Trusts and Other Ways to Avoid Probate (3E)	$24.95	
	1-57248-349-0	The Antique and Art Collector's Legal Guide	$24.95			1-57248-186-2	Manual de Beneficios para el Seguro Social	$18.95	
	1-57248-347-4	Attroney Responsibilities & Client Rights	$19.95			1-57248-220-6	Mastering the MBE	$16.95	
	1-57248-148-X	Cómo Hacer su Propio Testamento	$16.95			1-57248-167-6	Most Val. Business Legal Forms You'll Ever Need (3E)	$21.95	
	1-57248-226-5	Cómo Restablecer su propio Crédito y Renegociar sus Deudas	$21.95			1-57248-360-1	Most Val. Personal Legal Forms You'll Ever Need (2E)	$26.95	
	1-57248-147-1	Cómo Solicitar su Propio Divorcio	$24.95			1-57248-098-X	The Nanny and Domestic Help Legal Kit	$22.95	
	1-57248-166-8	The Complete Book of Corporate Forms	$24.95			1-57248-089-0	Neighbor v. Neighbor (2E)	$16.95	
	1-57248-353-9	The Complete Kit to Selling Your Own Home	$18.95			1-57248-388-1	The Power of Attorney Handbook (5E)	$22.95	
	1-57248-229-X	The Complete Legal Guide to Senior Care	$21.95			1-57248-332-6	Profit from Intellectual Property	$28.95	
	1-57248-391-1	The Complete Partnership Book	$24.95			1-57248-329-6	Protect Your Patent	$24.95	
	1-57248-201-X	The Complete Patent Book	$26.95			1-57248-385-7	Quick Cash	$14.95	
	1-57248-369-5	Credit Smart	$18.95			1-57248-344-X	Repair Your Own Credit and Deal with Debt (2E)	$18.95	
	1-57248-163-3	Crime Victim's Guide to Justice (2E)	$21.95			1-57248-350-4	El Seguro Social Preguntas y Respuestas	$14.95	
	1-57248-367-9	Employees' Rights	$18.95			1-57248-217-6	Sexual Harassment: Your Guide to Legal Action	$18.95	
	1-57248-365-2	Employer's Rights	$24.95			1-57248-219-2	The Small Business Owner's Guide to Bankruptcy	$21.95	
	1-57248-251-6	The Entrepreneur's Internet Handbook	$21.95			1-57248-168-4	The Social Security Benefits Handbook (3E)	$18.95	
	1-57248-235-4	The Entrepreneur's Legal Guide	$26.95			1-57248-216-8	Social Security Q&A	$12.95	
	1-57248-346-6	Essential Guide to Real Estate Contracts (2E)	$18.95			1-57248-221-4	Teen Rights	$22.95	
	1-57248-160-9	Essential Guide to Real Estate Leases	$18.95			1-57248-366-0	Tax Smarts for Small Business	$21.95	
	1-57248-254-0	Family Limited Partnership	$26.95			1-57248-335-0	Traveler's Rights	$21.95	
	1-57248-331-8	Gay & Lesbian Rights	$26.95			1-57248-236-2	Unmarried Parents' Rights (2E)	$19.95	
	1-57248-139-0	Grandparents' Rights (3E)	$24.95			1-57248-362-8	U.S. Immigration and Citizenship Q&A	$16.95	
	1-57248-188-9	Guía de Inmigración a Estados Unidos (3E)	$24.95			1-57248-387-3	U.S. Immigration Step by Step (2E)	$24.95	
	1-57248-187-0	Guía de Justicia para Víctimas del Crimen	$21.95			1-57248-392-X	U.S.A. Immigration Guide (5E)	$26.95	
	1-57248-253-2	Guía Esencial para los Contratos de Arrendamiento de Bienes Raices	$22.95			1-57248-192-7	The Visitation Handbook	$18.95	
	1-57248-103-X	Help Your Lawyer Win Your Case (2E)	$14.95			1-57248-225-7	Win Your Unemployment Compensation Claim (2E)	$21.95	
	1-57248-334-2	Homeowner's Rights	$21.95			1-57248-330-X	The Wills, Estate Planning and Trusts Legal Kit	&26.95	
	1-57248-164-1	How to Buy a Condominium or Townhome (2E)	$19.95			1-57248-138-2	Winning Your Personal Injury Claim (2E)	$24.95	
	1-57248-328-8	How to Buy Your First Home	$18.95			1-57248-333-4	Working with Your Homeowners Association	$19.95	
	1-57248-191-9	How to File Your Own Bankruptcy (5E)	$21.95			1-57248-380-6	Your Right to Child Custody, Visitation and Support (3E)	$24.95	
	1-57248-343-1	How to File Your Own Divorce (5E)	$26.95			1-57248-157-9	Your Rights When You Owe Too Much	$16.95	
	1-57248-222-2	How to Form a Limited Liability Company (2E)	$24.95				**CALIFORNIA TITLES**		
	1-57248-231-1	How to Form a Nonprofit Corporation (2E)	$24.95			1-57248-150-1	CA Power of Attorney Handbook (2E)	$18.95	
	1-57248-345-8	How to Form Your Own Corporation (4E)	$26.95			1-57248-337-7	How to File for Divorce in CA (4E)	$26.95	
	1-57248-232-X	How to Make Your Own Simple Will (3E)	$18.95			1-57248-145-5	How to Probate and Settle an Estate in CA	$26.95	
	1-57248-379-2	How to Register Your Own Copyright (5E)	$24.95			1-57248-336-9	How to Start a Business in CA (2E)	$21.95	
	1-57248-104-8	How to Register Your Own Trademark (3E)	$21.95			1-57248-194-3	How to Win in Small Claims Court in CA (2E)	$18.95	
	1-57248-233-8	How to Write Your Own Living Will (3E)	$18.95			1-57248-246-X	Make Your Own CA Will	$18.95	
	1-57248-156-0	How to Write Your Own Premarital Agreement (3E)	$24.95			1-57248-196-X	The Landlord's Legal Guide in CA	$24.95	
	1-57248-230-3	Incorporate in Delaware from Any State	$26.95			1-57248-241-9	Tenants' Rights in CA	$21.95	
	1-57248-158-7	Incorporate in Nevada from Any State	$24.95						
	1-57248-250-8	Inmigración a los EE.UU. Paso a Paso	$22.95						
	1-57071-333-2	Jurors' Rights (2E)	$12.95						
	1-57248-374-1	Law School 101	$16.95				**Form Continued on Following Page**	**SubTotal**	

SPHINX® PUBLISHING ORDER FORM

Qty	ISBN	Title	Retail	Ext.
		FLORIDA TITLES		
___	1-57071-363-4	Florida Power of Attorney Handbook (2E)	$16.95	___
___	1-57248-396-2	How to File for Divorce in FL (8E)	$28.95	___
___	1-57248-356-3	How to Form a Corporation in FL (6E)	$24.95	___
___	1-57248-203-6	How to Form a Limited Liability Co. in FL (2E)	$24.95	___
___	1-57071-401-0	How to Form a Partnership in FL	$22.95	___
___	1-57248-113-7	How to Make a FL Will (6E)	$16.95	___
___	1-57248-088-2	How to Modify Your FL Divorce Judgment (4E)	$24.95	___
___	1-57248-354-7	How to Probate and Settle an Estate in FL (5E)	$26.95	___
___	1-57248-339-3	How to Start a Business in FL (7E)	$21.95	___
___	1-57248-204-4	How to Win in Small Claims Court in FL (7E)	$18.95	___
___	1-57248-381-4	Land Trusts in Florida (7E)	$29.95	___
___	1-57248-338-5	Landlords' Rights and Duties in FL (9E)	$22.95	___
		GEORGIA TITLES		
___	1-57248-340-7	How to File for Divorce in GA (5E)	$21.95	___
___	1-57248-180-3	How to Make a GA Will (4E)	$21.95	___
___	1-57248-341-5	How to Start a Business in Georgia (3E)	$21.95	___
		ILLINOIS TITLES		
___	1-57248-244-3	Child Custody, Visitation, and Support in IL	$24.95	___
___	1-57248-206-0	How to File for Divorce in IL (3E)	$24.95	___
___	1-57248-170-6	How to Make an IL Will (3E)	$16.95	___
___	1-57248-247-8	How to Start a Business in IL (3E)	$21.95	___
___	1-57248-252-4	The Landlord's Legal Guide in IL	$24.95	___
		MARYLAND, VIRGINIA AND THE DISTRICT OF COLUMBIA		
___	1-57248-240-0	How to File for Divorce in MD, VA and DC	$28.95	___
___	1-57248-359-8	How to Start a Business in MD, VA or DC	$21.95	___
		MASSACHUSETTS TITLES		
___	1-57248-128-5	How to File for Divorce in MA (3E)	$24.95	___
___	1-57248-115-3	How to Form a Corporation in MA	$24.95	___
___	1-57248-108-0	How to Make a MA Will (2E)	$16.95	___
___	1-57248-248-6	How to Start a Business in MA (3E)	$21.95	___
___	1-57248-209-5	The Landlord's Legal Guide in MA	$24.95	___
		MICHIGAN TITLES		
___	1-57248-215-X	How to File for Divorce in MI (3E)	$24.95	___
___	1-57248-182-X	How to Make a MI Will (3E)	$16.95	___
___	1-57248-183-8	How to Start a Business in MI (3E)	$18.95	___
		MINNESOTA TITLES		
___	1-57248-142-0	How to File for Divorce in MN	$21.95	___
___	1-57248-179-X	How to Form a Corporation in MN	$24.95	___
___	1-57248-178-1	How to Make a MN Will (2E)	$16.95	___
		NEW JERSEY TITLES		
___	1-57248-239-7	How to File for Divorce in NJ	$24.95	___
		NEW YORK TITLES		
___	1-57248-193-5	Child Custody, Visitation and Support in NY	$26.95	___
___	1-57248-351-2	File for Divorce in NY	$26.95	___
___	1-57248-249-4	How to Form a Corporation in NY (2E)	$24.95	___
___	1-57248-401-2	How to Make a NY Will (3E)	$16.95	___
___	1-57248-199-4	How to Start a Business in NY (2E)	$18.95	___
___	1-57248-198-6	How to Win in Small Claims Court in NY (2E)	$18.95	___
___	1-57248-197-8	Landlords' Legal Guide in NY	$24.95	___
___	1-57071-188-7	New York Power of Attorney Handbook	$19.95	___
___	1-57248-122-6	Tenants' Rights in NY	$21.95	___
		NORTH CAROLINA TITLES		
___	1-57248-185-4	How to File for Divorce in NC (3E)	$22.95	___
___	1-57248-129-3	How to Make a NC Will (3E)	$16.95	___
___	1-57248-184-6	How to Start a Business in NC (3E)	$18.95	___
___	1-57248-091-2	Landlords' Rights & Duties in NC	$21.95	___
		NORTH CAROLINA AND SOUTH CAROLINA TITLES		
___	1-57248-371-7	How to Start a Business in NC or SC	$24.95	___
		OHIO TITLES		
___	1-57248-190-0	How to File for Divorce in OH (2E)	$24.95	___
___	1-57248-174-9	How to Form a Corporation in OH	$24.95	___
___	1-57248-173-0	How to Make an OH Will	$16.95	___
		PENNSYLVANIA TITLES		
___	1-57248-242-7	Child Custody, Visitation and Support in PA	$26.95	___
___	1-57248-211-7	How to File for Divorce in PA (3E)	$26.95	___
___	1-57248-358-X	How to Form a Croporation in PA	$24.95	___
___	1-57248-094-7	How to Make a PA Will (2E)	$16.95	___
___	1-57248-357-1	How to Start a Business in PA (3E)	$21.95	___
___	1-57248-245-1	The Landlord's Legal Guide in PA	$24.95	___
		TEXAS TITLES		
___	1-57248-171-4	Child Custody, Visitation, and Support in TX	$22.95	___
___	1-57248-399-7	How to File for Divorce in TX (4E)	$24.95	___
___	1-57248-114-5	How to Form a Corporation in TX (2E)	$24.95	___
___	1-57248-255-9	How to Make a TX Will (3E)	$16.95	___
___	1-57248-214-1	How to Probate and Settle an Estate in TX (3E)	$26.95	___
___	1-57248-228-1	How to Start a Business in TX (3E)	$18.95	___
___	1-57248-111-0	How to Win in Small Claims Court in TX (2E)	$16.95	___
___	1-57248-355-5	The Landlord's Legal Guide in TX	$24.95	___

SubTotal This page ___

SubTotal previous page ___

Shipping— $5.00 for 1st book, $1.00 each additional ___

Illinois residents add 6.75% sales tax ___

Connecticut residents add 6.00% sales tax ___

Total_ ___

To order, call Sourcebooks at 1-800-432-7444 or FAX (630) 961-2168 (Bookstores, libraries, wholesalers—please call for discount)

Prices are subject to change without notice.

Find more legal information at: **www.SphinxLegal.com**